T0334112

The Role of Student Affairs in Advancing Community College Student Success

This collection brings together insightful chapters which explore diverse student success initiatives and programs in response to challenges faced by community colleges.

Each chapter of the collection magnifies a specific aspect of student affairs to illustrate how dedicated departments and practitioners have effectively supported student success via select projects or initiatives. Readers will gain a deeper insight into the contemporary applications, practices, and impacts of agendas such as the assessment of student affairs and services, student success programming, Guided Pathways, and The Completion Agenda. By demonstrating the meaningful involvement of student affairs practitioners in fulfilling institutional missions and visions, this collection contributes to an overarching dialogue about promoting community college student success.

This collection will be of interest to researchers, academics, graduates, and postgraduate students in the fields of higher education administration, educational leadership, adult education, and lifelong learning.

C. Casey Ozaki is Associate Professor of Education, Health, and Human Behavior Studies at the University of North Dakota, USA.

Paulette Dalpes is Vice President of Student Affairs at the Community College of Aurora, USA.

Deborah L. Floyd is Professor of Higher Education, Educational Leadership and Research Methodology at Florida Atlantic University, USA.

Gianna Ramdin is Associate Graduate Faculty and Adjunct Professor, Educational Leadership and Research Methodology at Florida Atlantic University, USA.

The Role of Student Affairs in Advancing Community College Student Success

An Examination of Selected Contemporary Initiatives

Edited by C. Casey Ozaki, Paulette Dalpes, Deborah L. Floyd, and Gianna Ramdin

Routledge
Taylor & Francis Group

NEW YORK AND LONDON

First published 2020
by Routledge
605 Third Avenue, New York, NY 10017

and by Routledge
2 Park Square, Milton Park, Abingdon, Oxon, OX14 4RN

First issued in paperback 2021

Routledge is an imprint of the Taylor & Francis Group, an informa business

Library of Congress Cataloging-in-Publication Data
A catalog record for this title has been requested

ISBN 13: 978-0-367-78786-8 (pbk)
ISBN 13: 978-0-367-23169-9 (hbk)

Typeset in Times New Roman
by codeMantra

Contents

1 Community College Student Affairs: Student Success Initiatives

Deborah L. Floyd, C. Casey Ozaki, Paulette Dalpes, and Gianna Ramdin

Community colleges have a storied history of providing access to relevant education and training for diverse student populations in local communities. Since the inception of the first community college (Joliet Junior College, Illinois) in 1901 (Cohen, Brawer, & Kisker, 2013), these institutions have expanded their scope and functions beyond the first two years of a four-year postsecondary education and embraced a sweeping commitment to student success in and out of the classroom. As community college curricular offerings have expanded, so have programs and efforts to ensure students' well-being, development, and success.

Evolving Terminology and Programs

Terminology has evolved over the years as junior colleges became community colleges and some are now referring to themselves as state colleges. Similarly, terminology has evolved in the field of Student Affairs. By the 1970s the term Student Personnel was replaced with more descriptive denotations, such as Student Affairs and Student Services, to specifically communicate the organizational role of Student Affairs as an administrative sector and its departmental functions that contributed to the development of the whole student (Crookston, 1976). During the 1980s and 1990s, Student Affairs professionals led efforts to recognize achievement gaps related to graduation among certain student demographic cohorts and marshaled greater attention and resources to students' first-year experiences (Venit, 2016). Present-day practices of using early alert technologies combined with concerns over rising tuition costs have reemphasized graduate rates and highlighted long-term degree planning, which has allowed Student Affairs professionals to translate first-year retention achievements into degree completion (Venit, 2016).

By the last two decades of the 20th century, Student Affairs services and programs had expanded to multidimensional efforts focusing on ensuring student success in and out of the classroom. Terminology reflected these changes as some units were called *Student Development Services* and *Student Success Programs*. Student Affairs in community colleges focuses on student services and academic support for student success in contrast with university Student Affairs that can include residential life programming and other activities such as Greek life.

Thus, over the years as their leadership and influence shifted from a service to a holistic development and student success orientation, terminology evolved. Student Affairs units utilized various terms describing their units such as *Student Development* and *Student Success*.

Looking back at numerous initiatives and eras, community college Student Affairs professionals have embraced challenges of advocating for students and have led the charge toward focusing on ways the institution can better align services, programs, and initiatives toward student success goals. Savvy Student Affairs leaders model the way by continuously examining programmatic and policy issues as they impact student matriculation and success.

Student Success: Context and Contemporary Initiatives

Student Affairs professionals know that for students to truly be successful, they must be able to compete in a global world. Today, unfortunately, postsecondary education in the United States has lagged behind other countries' graduation and educational outcomes (Lumina Foundation, 2015; OECD, 2014; Pell Institute for the Study of Economic Opportunity, 2011) and struggled to make substantial improvements to its college graduation rates for years (Lewin, 2010; Lumina, 2015). This has maintained the attention of researchers, administrators, and policy-makers alike in their shared concern that the United States is losing its competitive edge educationally in a global competition and is failing to educate the workforce with 21st-century knowledge and skills. Increasingly, jobs offering sustainable living wages will require some postsecondary credential.

Today, as a result of increasing expectations for accountability and measurable outcomes, critical initiatives and trends to create organizational change and greater accountability for student learning and success have been launched, especially within community colleges. Examples of these efforts include: Guided Pathways, the Completion Agenda, America's College Promise, assessment of student outcomes, predictive analytics, implementation of new technologies, and performance-based funding. These trends and initiatives are shaping the ways students are served, assessments are implemented, resources are allocated, and, at times, how higher education institutions are organized to address these needed changes.

Research supports that critical elements for student success include educational experiences outside the classroom (Kuh, Kinzie, Schuh, & Whitt, 2005; Pascarella & Terenzini, 2005), such as co-curricular activities involving student activities and government, athletics, and service learning. Every touch point of a student's experience provides opportunities to influence success or create barriers to completion. From the point of outreach and recruitment, application, financial aid, enrollment and registration, every connection must be meaningful, sustainable, and guide the student with the end in mind. In addition, other academic and support services including advising, career services, counseling, tutoring, and supplemental instruction are designed to support the student to completion. Co-curricular experiences and services influence students' sense of belonging, ease in navigating the institution, and ability and motivation to persist when challenges arise (Pascarella & Terenzini, 2005). Given the high population of underserved students at community colleges and high departure rates (American Association of Community Colleges [AACC], 2016; Cohen et al., 2013), the importance of these experiences and services is especially critical. Student Affairs leaders and Student Services personnel are generally considered the design, implementation, and managing experts regarding these critical experiences. Therefore, the role of these professionals in supporting and advancing student success is foundational.

As significant aspects of the institution, it is reasonable that Student Affairs is also expected to respond to calls for student success and related initiatives and trends. Yet, while there has been plenty of research and discussion about national, state, and institutional initiatives and trends, very little of this literature examines how they are implemented and how they influence Student Affairs and Student Services practice, programs, and work. Recent books focused on Student Affairs and working with students in community colleges (Kelsay & Zamani-Gallaher, 2014; Tull, Kuk, & Dalpes, 2015) are more holistic and comprehensive in their approach. Less literature is available specific to how community college Student Affairs and Student Services are responding to particular student success-driven trends and initiatives. Jamrogowicz (2013) explored the relevance of the American Graduation Initiative for community colleges and Phillips and Horowitz (2013) edited a *New Directions for Community Colleges* volume addressing approaches for reaching the College Completion Agenda. While these community college published works focus on the implementation approaches of Student Affairs initiatives, they did not examine Student Affairs or Student Services' responses to these initiatives. Furthermore, much of the literature that is available appears to be scholarly and practice-focused versus empirically based. Given the lack of focus and visibility of community colleges in the literature, even more opaque and unclear are the impact and responses of community college Student Affairs and Student Services to student success initiatives and trends.

In this collection, empirical research, case studies, and scholarly commentary are used to provide depth and breadth to this conversation. These papers build on a historical foundation by exploring and examining selected contemporary student success initiatives and trends that are shaping the student experiences on community college campuses today. First, Kimberly Lowry, Dawna Wilson Horton, and Karen Stills Royster described the stories of two community colleges' development of assessment capacity and implementation within Student Affairs and support services. Following, Jason L. Taylor and Chuck W. Lepper examine Salt Lake Community College's new Promise program, designed to make college more affordable, and the role of Student Affairs in its design and implementation. The article closes with an examination of the program's first-year outcomes. While Taylor and Lepper examine a promise program at one institution, William Watson, Adela Esquivel-Swinson, and Roland Montemayor discuss a community college district's effort to grow its capacity to serve immigrant populations through the implementation of required and elective collaborative change initiatives, specifically a consortium of five adult schools and four community colleges, and professional development for Student Services staff. David J. Nguyen, G. Blue Brazelton, Kristen A. Renn, and Michael R. Woodford focus on a specific population, LGBTQ+ students on community colleges, examining the availability of support services through a mixed methods study. Patrick W. Gill and Laura M. Harrison broaden their work to a qualitative study of the possible challenges and benefits of the Completion Agenda on Student Affairs practice in community colleges. In a scholarly article,

Michael A. Baston uses Rassen, Chaplot, Jenkins, and Johnstone's (2013) Loss/Momentum Framework to inform efforts to redesign campus environments, the development of guided pathways, and advance institutional change. Finally, Anne M. Hornak, C. Casey Ozaki, Amanda O. Latz, and Dan W. Royer examine the implications for Student Affairs professionals at community colleges in the era of the Trump administration.

No doubt, community college Student Affairs have a splendid history of making a difference in students' lives and modeling the way for organizational change. While the history of community college Student Affairs is impressive, we are delighted that history is being made every day as innovative, creative, and talented professionals implement campus-based initiatives designed to foster student success. The papers that follow contribute to documenting history by providing readers an overview of some current initiatives and trends designed to foster student success in hopes that this will stimulate dialogue and action that continues the improvement of programs. Our hope is that this collection of readings will serve as a practical and empirical catalyst for conversation about a topic at the core of the community college mission—student success.

References

American Association of Community Colleges. (2016, February). *2016 fast facts*. Washington, DC: American Association of Community Colleges. Retrieved from http://www.aacc.nche.edu/AboutCC/Documents/AACC FactSheetsR2.pdf.

Cohen, A. M., Brawer, F. B., & Kisker, C. B. (2013). *The American community college* (6th ed.). San Francisco, CA: Jossey Bass.

Crookston, B. (1976). Student personnel—all hail and farewell! *Personnel and Guidance Journal, 55*, 26–29.

Jamrogowicz, J. L. (2013). Community college economic climate, policy landscape, and the American Graduation Initiative. In L. S. Kelsay & E. M. Zamani-Gallaher (Eds.), *Working with students in community colleges: Contemporary strategies for bridging theory, research, and practice* (pp. 17–30). Sterling, VA: Stylus.

Kelsay, L. S., & Zamani-Gallaher, E. M. (Eds.). (2014). *Working with students in community colleges: Contemporary strategies for bridging theory, research, and practice*. Sterling, VA: Stylus.

Kuh, G. D., Kinzie, J., Schuh, J. H., & Whitt, E. J. (2005). *Student success in college: Creating conditions that matter*. Washington, DC: Jossey-Bass.

Lewin, T. (2010, July 23). Once a leader, U.S. lags in college degrees. *New York Times*. Retrieved from http://www.nytimes.com/2010/07/23/education/23college.html?_r=0

Lumina Foundation. (2015). *Goal 2025*. Indianapolis, IN: Author. Retrieved from http://www.luminafoundation.org/ goal_2025

OECD. (2014). *Education at a glance 2014: OECD Indicators*. Paris: Author.

Pascarella, E. T., & Terenzini, P. T. (2005). *How college affects students. Vol. 2. A third decade of research*. San Francisco, CA: Jossey-Bass.

Pell Institute for the Study of Economic Opportunity. (2011). *Developing 20/20 vision on the 2020 degree attainment goal*. Washington, DC: Author. Retrieved from http://www.pellinstitute.org/downloads/publications-Developing_ 2020_Vision_May_2011.pdf

Phillips, B. C., & Horowitz, J. E. (2013, Winter). The college completion agenda: Practical approaches for reaching the big goal. *New Directions for Community Colleges, 2013*(164), 17–25.

Rassen, E., Chaplot, P., Jenkins, P. D., & Johnstone, R. (2013). *Understanding the student experience through the loss/momentum framework: Clearing the path to completion*. Berkeley, CA: RP Group. Retrieved from https://ccrc.tc.columbia.edu/media/k2/attachments/understanding-student-experience-cbd.pdf

Tull, A., Kuk, L., & Dalpes, P. (2015). *Handbook for student affairs in community colleges*. Sterling, VA: Stylus.

Venit, E. (2016). *The evolution of student success*. Retrieved from https://www.eab.com/technology/student-success-collaborative/members/infographics/the-evolution-of-student-success

2 Building Student Affairs Assessment Capacity: Lessons from Two Community Colleges

Kimberly Lowry, Dawna Wilson Horton, and Karen Stills Royster

High-quality Student Affairs programming and support services are indispensable to community college student success. Yet, while institutions establish well-structured assessment of academic programs, few engage in formal institutional measurement of Student Affairs and Services effectiveness. A critical early step in formalizing Student Affairs assessment involves laying a foundation that promotes best practices and courts institution-wide buy-in. The purpose of this article is to share two community colleges' stories of building assessment capacity within Student Affairs divisions. Eastfield College journeyed from identifying a need to make data-informed decisions for continuous improvement to laying a foundation of ongoing structured assessment. El Centro College's path began with developing staff and establishing buy-in to conduct assessments across Student Affairs departments and inspiring other campus divisions to follow suit.

Building Capacity

A continuous improvement strategy, building capacity or capacity building often refers to an organization's efforts to enhance its ability to accomplish its stated mission and goals (Beckhard, 1969). Bentrim and Henning (2015) defined capacity building as "the intentional and planned development of an increase in skills or knowledge or allowing organizations or individuals to fulfill their mission in the most effective and productive manner" (p. 1). For Student Affairs assessment leaders, key players in influencing culture change, building capacity serves as a means of preparing organizations to establish and cultivate an evidence-based culture. Within Student Affairs divisions, building capacity not only involves training staff but establishing assessment practices that yield data to inform decision-making and continuous improvement. Duncan and Holmes (2015) outlined five components of building capacity with students affairs: (1) leading conversations about assessment "why's" and "how's"; (2) securing commitment to a culture change; (3) providing consistent support through the change; (4) creating connections among those doing the assessment work as well as among institutional units; and (5) facilitating effective communication about assessment, outcomes, and change among stakeholders. Though Bentrim and Henning state, "building a culture of assessment and establishing the organizational attitude can be arduous at times" (p. 4), efforts can yield clear measures of Student Affairs ' contributions to the institution's mission and goals.

Literature Review

Student Affairs Assessment

Assessment of student learning dates as far back as teaching (Yousey-Elsener, Bentrim, & Henning, 2015). Mid-20th-century expansion of student development theory helped launch exploration of student experiences and laid a foundation for assessment (Henning & Roberts, 2016). According to Ewell (2002), amid growing accountability demands, 1980s marked an increase in scholarly examinations of how higher education assessed student growth and achievement. Subsequently, the 1990s saw accreditation bodies emphasize the development and measurement of student learning outcomes (Yousey-Elsener et al., 2015). Student Affairs assessment, in turn, emerged from the need to measure student experiences outside the classroom.

Research by student development scholars demonstrates a clear link between the services and programs Student Affairs provides and student success (Astin, 1993; Pascarella & Terenzini, 2005; Schuh & Gansemer-Topf, 2010). For example, Whitt (2005) concluded,

> the contribution of out-of-class experiences to student engagement cannot be overstated. Any institution that wishes to make student achievement, satisfaction, persistence, and learning a priority must have competent Student Affairs professionals whose contributions complement the academic mission of the institution in ways that help students and the institution realize their goals.
>
> (p. 1)

Given the significance of Student Affairs to overall student success, internal and external higher education stakeholders rightly ask, "How do we know Student Affairs practices affect change, benefit students, and promote completion?" In other words, how does Student Affairs demonstrate effectiveness? What measures provide these answers?

Bresciani, Gardner, and Hickmott (2009) stated that the purpose of Student Affairs assessment is to "demonstrate the significant contributions that co-curricular experiences have on student learning and development" (p. 138). Often compelled by limited resources, Student Affairs departments must increasingly display a return on investment and produce documented proof that the services they provide do indeed make a positive difference in students' collegiate experiences. Today, assessment is a vital component of Student Affairs' ability to demonstrate effectiveness, operate with limited resources, evidence accountability to internal and external stakeholders, allocate and plan and most importantly, inform continuous improvement (Palomba & Banta, 1999). However, far too often, higher education institutions cannot find themselves at the first stage of assessing Student Affairs–building capacity.

Eastfield's Story

At the first stage of building capacity is precisely where Eastfield College (EFC) stood in spring 2015 when it initiated efforts to implement Student Affairs assessment. A public two-year community college serving the eastern Dallas County region, EFC routinely enrolls one-fifth of all Dallas County Community College District students. In fall 2016, enrollment numbered just over 15,000. Prior to spring 2015, EFC practiced limited reviews of Student Affairs department and activities. Apart from infrequent student comments submitted via paper feedback forms, the college conducted no formal assessment regarding the effectiveness of support services areas. Input from students and staff, although welcomed, was neither formally nor systematically solicited or analyzed.

The Need

In spring 2015, led by a newly appointed student services administrator, EFC sought to improve operations within support services by aligning procedures with best practices. The first step was to determine how departments were operating and then review how services contributed to student success. The administrator met with directors of academic advising, dual credit, early college high school, and veteran services and asked two questions: (1), "What is your department doing to support student success at EFC?" and (2) "How do you know your efforts are working?" The administrator quickly discovered an absence of structured planning based on goals and objectives. In fact, when departments attempted to answer the questions, they realized that they had collected no data to determine the effectiveness of processes, procedures, and programs or their impact on student success. These findings, coupled with growing budgetary constraints, prompted the administrator to launch efforts to build assessment capacity within those departments.

Plan of Action

After realizing that a foundation for assessment did not exist, the Student Services administrator set out to construct a plan of action with no external funding and a limited budget. Utilizing available resources, a research analyst whose work had been dedicated to grant specific data analysis and assessment within Student Services helped to design and implement an action plan. The ultimate purpose was to:

- Align student support services' practices with EFC's mission and goals
- Incorporate best practices based on national standards
- Move toward more data-informed decision-making
- Determine opportunities for continuous improvement
- Build in assessment as part of routine departmental practices
- Establish a standardized accountability system

To translate the implementation plan into practice, the administrator met with the respective directors of the targeted departments to outline the plan and its purpose while providing foundational training on assessment. Once the framework was set, each director was charged with setting measurable departmental goals and objectives. The Council for the Advancement of Standards in Higher Education (CAS) standards were introduced to help the directors with scope and provide context. The CAS Standards also guided directors through designing appropriate assessments while highlighting best practices.

In fall 2015, the implementation plan was put into action, and the research analyst, who had helped design the plan, was identified as the lead facilitator. Previously, the research analyst had been solely dedicated to grant-related work in a split-funded position (50% grant funded and 50% institution funded) resulting in the analyst being assigned to help with this project in addition to the work that was being done for the grant. The research analyst then began to meet with directors providing additional training, support, and guidance throughout fall 2015. More specifically, the analyst individually walked directors through setting measurable departmental goals and objectives. The analyst also introduced directors to CAS Standards and how to use them when writing goals and building assessments. To inform departments for which CAS Standards did not exist, the analyst consulted principles from professional associations and national organization affiliated with those departments' functions.

Outcomes

Similar to any organization seeking to build capacity, EFC experienced successes and challenges. As for successes, building assessment capacity within the specific student services areas not only resulted in all four departments establishing measurable goals and objectives with aligned assessments by spring 2016, but it impacted the entire division. Deans and directors throughout support services engaged in more frequent conversations about assessment. In fact, several initiated their own efforts to assess their specific areas. But perhaps the most significant outcome was the formalization of assessing peak registration. Since fall 2015, each semester EFC has collected data on student and staff experiences with peak registration via an online student survey and student and staff focus groups. In response to this data, support services has:

- Established student learning outcomes for all offices/ departments
- Established cross-departmental teams to plan, implement, and review peak registration
- Reduced student registration barriers
- Increased staff contributions to continuous improvement
- Increased staff buy-in regarding assessment

Yet, despite successes, challenges were encountered. The greatest challenge was neither the implementation of the assessment process nor support from senior administration, but buy-in from directors and staff. Despite ongoing support and guidance, the involved directors resisted the idea of department assessment. They, along with their staff, equated department assessment with performance evaluation. This misperception prompted directors to repeatedly set inappropriate or "safe" goals during the goal-setting phase to ensure their goals would be met. Additionally, during data review and analysis, directors would routinely underreport outcomes sharing only positive outcomes rather than all outcomes. Since student satisfaction surveys represented the data collection instrument with which directors were most familiar, another challenge was shifting directors from customer service only measures to assessing student learning. Limited time emerged as a challenge as well. Because EFC sought to build capacity during the fall semester, directors were occupied with their duties and had little extra time to devote to learning the assessment process. Further, most were being asked for the first time in their Student Affairs careers to assess their areas, so they needed ample time to "buy-in" and grasp the process. The final challenge was convincing directors and staff that assessment was an effective means of revealing what was going well and what could be improved. In other words, assessment was simply a means to an end, and that end was continuous improvement.

Lessons Learned

Eastfield learned a number of important lessons from its initial efforts to institute Student Affairs assessment. Among the most significant were to:

- Allow enough time to secure "buy-in" and reduce resistance among staff implementing assessment measures
- Adequately prepare and train staff for the assessment process
- Make a clear distinction between department assessment and employee evaluation
- Acknowledge that despite continuous support, resistance and misconceptions may linger
- Effectively communicate how results inform continuous improvement

Though EFC did not achieve all of its intended implementation goals, the college has moved the needle in the right direction.

Student services staff across the division now routinely discuss assessment. Further, recognizing the need for additional capacity building, administrators have strategically prioritized assessment and ardently support efforts to build a culture of evidence throughout student services.

El Centro's Story

El Centro College (ECC), the flagship college of the Dallas County Community College District, currently serves over 10,000 students in the downtown Dallas region. During the last decade, the community college agenda has shifted from solely *access* to *access* and *credential completion*. Likewise, community college funding sources have increasingly aligned with credential completion. For example, in Texas, 10% of state funding for community colleges is linked to completion rates with plans to increase this percentage over time. Based on the completion agenda, ECC has comprehensively reconsidered how they serve students.

The Need

Within Student Affairs, the college had to look beyond enrollment and student satisfaction and delve into strategies that successfully onboard and guide students toward credential completion. To inform strategic improvement discussions, ECC student services had to first assess where they were as a unit. An evaluation of services revealed that program assessment varied among departments. Varied levels of understanding among department leaders about program assessment highlighted a need to build assessment capacity. For example, some departments administered service satisfaction, while others had no established standard baseline by which to measure improvement. Further, when trying to assess procedures and protocols used to serve students, ECC discovered that many departments did not have up-to-date operational guidelines or manuals that detailed current strategies or practices to serve students. Some departments did not have operational manuals at all. These discoveries illuminated an urgent need for the ECC Student Services and Enrollment Management division to conduct a comprehensive evaluation of its programs and services, so that it could make informed strategies for improvement.

Plan of Action

In summer 2015, the Student Services and Enrollment Management (SSEM) division applied for and received an internal institutional grant, the Circles of Excellence Award, funded by ECC's Office of the President. Grant recipients implemented action plans for continuous quality improvement throughout the campus. Based on their action plan, SSEM undertook a yearlong, self-study project to evaluate 17 different departments, student programs, and services including recruitment, outreach, admissions, testing, advising, the multicultural center, student life, counseling, student veteran services, disability services, and career services. To encourage meaningful participation, the project recognized and awarded three milestone incentives:

- Milestone 1 (Bronze): Reached after completing a departmental assessment both individually and as part of a team; awarded with cookie delivery to departmental office
- Milestone 2 (Silver): Reached after developing a departmental action plan based on CAS assessment results; awarded with "Comp Time Coupon" redeemable for 1 hour of professional development or wellness in lieu of personal vacation time
- Milestone 3 (Gold): Reached after demonstrating implementation of departmental action plan; awarded with (1) special lapel pin, (2) invitation to recognition luncheon, highlighting departmental work and commitment to continuous improvement, and (3) departmental APPEX: Advancing Procedure and Protocol Excellence Golden Standard of Excellence designation.

The project, named APPEX: *Advancing Procedure and Protocol Excellence*, specifically aimed to evaluate student services programs and document procedures and ultimately improve operational protocols. APPEX' expected outcomes were to:

- Help student service areas to determine where to focus time, energy, and resources
- Reflect on and measure current programmatic and operational delivery of services
- Document clear and concise procedures and protocols
- Guide department and division strategic planning as the college embarks on a new institutional strategic plan

- Evaluate and/or develop program, operational, and student outcomes
- Develop related staff development training plan

APPEX used the Council for the Advancement of Standards in Higher Education (CAS) as its evaluative framework. Established to develop and promote professional standards for higher education practitioners, CAS Standards provided clear guidelines for assessing ECC's programs and services.

In fall 2015, project administrators acquired and reviewed CAS materials, identified a self-study leadership team, and mapped out an action plan and implementation schedule. The action plan outlined a task timeline, a branding and communication plan, and three distinct milestones with completion incentives. Spring 2016 marked the implementation phase of APPEX. Project leaders trained student services staff, faculty, and students on what CAS Standards were and how to use CAS assessment guides. Initial APPEX action steps included developing an APPEX logo, creating introductory training materials, and reviewing department procedures and protocols. In line with CAS guidelines, evaluation teams were composed of students, instructional partners, and student services staff from areas outside of the departments being evaluated. This composition also ensured objectivity. Utilizing individual input to develop a collective rating, each team evaluated two departments. Team members scored 12 departmental areas that included: mission; program; organization and leadership; human resources; ethics; law, policy and governance; diversity, equity, and access; institutional and external relations; financial resources; technology; facilities, and equipment; and assessment and evaluation. Participants used CAS' six-scaled measurement ranging from "does not apply (0)" to "exceeds (3)" to rate each criterion. Ratings were synthesized and used to provide collective scores as well as written feedback and recommendations.

By August 2016, each evaluated student service area was expected to have an improvement action plan prepared for fall 2016 implementation. Furthermore, each area had to invite an external evaluation of CAS Standards at the completion of the departmental CAS self-study, provide training to implement procedures and protocols, and continue data-driven evaluations to make improvements.

Outcomes

Project APPEX proved highly effective in program evaluation, planning, assessment, and process improvement within the SSEM Division. Overall, it expanded opportunities to reflect on current operations and generated innovative strategies to address inefficient processes and protocols. Just as important, it prompted efforts to document procedures and staff development. As the SSEM Division communicated to the college improvement efforts, other areas, including instruction, dual credit, and the learning center, began to evaluate their processes. ECC went on to identify "process improvement" as a targeted focus area for our renewed Achieving the Dream strategic plan. Specific accomplishments included aligning student support services' practices with the institutional mission and goals, improvement in institutional processes, and implementing best practices aligned with national standards. Furthermore, this assessment project not only helped SSEM areas to better determine where they should focus time, energy, and resource but also helped connect APPEX action plans with zero-based budget planning for fiscal year 2018. Every student service and enrollment services area completed improvement action plans by fall 2016. Participants responded positively to incentives, and 77% agreed that the APPEX project was a good use of their time.

A greater percentage (83%) agreed that the APPEX project positively contributed to their professional development as a student services practitioner. One-hundred percent of student services and enrollment management departments created updated process/procedure manuals by spring 2017, while 100% of student services and enrollment management leadership staff participated in at least two process improvement trainings for the 2015–2016 academic year.

Lessons Learned

Despite positive outcomes, ECC's self-study assessment project offered a number of lessons. For example, the project overwhelmed some staff members. More than a quarter (27%) of participants initially felt that the yearlong implementation timeline was aggressive or unreasonable given the significant time commitment. There was a significant time commitment involved in completing a

CAS self-study that created a number of time management issues for participants. Also, because of the relational structure between the institution and the District office, participants felt that some of the professional standards included within the self-study were outside of their locus of control (i.e., hiring processes; financial aid processing). There were disconnects between establishing protocols/ procedures and actually implementing them on a consistent basis. An ongoing need to train coordinators and supervisors on building in regular assessment and evaluation strategies was identified. There remains a need to create templates to bridge various assessment activities (e.g., ATD, Enrollment Management, Departmental Monthly Reports, SLO Assessment) to show how all of the evaluative work connects. Specific lessons learned were to:

- Allow enough time to adequately implement the assessment plan
- Tailor assessment instruments or guidelines to meet the specific organizational structure
- Design action plans for ease of implementation
- Provide ongoing training on the assessment process
- Make clear connections between assessment activities among student services area

Despite the noted challenges, ECC student services staff have significantly strengthened their overall assessment knowledge and skills after implementing Project APPEX. The lessons learned will be utilized to improve service to students and to inform the expansion of assessment practices across the division.

Conclusion

Moving the needle toward increased assessment of Student Affairs practices, procedures and activities represents a requisite step to validate not only Student Affairs' worth to student college experiences but ultimately its contribution to student completion. High-quality Student Affairs programming and support services are key factors in community college student success (Kuh, 2009). Yet, while these two-year institutions have well-established and structured assessment of academic programs, few engaged in formal institutional assessment of Student Affairs. Assessment provides an avenue for Student Affairs to measure and demonstrate its contribution to student success, remain accountable to internal and external stakeholders, and engage in continuous improvements. Further, Student Affairs assessment helps align student services practices with institutional mission, purpose, and strategic plan and contributes to campus-wide student learning outcomes assessment. Eastfield and El Centro Colleges learned valuable lessons in building assessment capacity within Student Affairs divisions. Their experiences have implications for the future of assessment within Student Affairs at community colleges. As a vital contributor to fulfilling institutional missions, Student Affairs must routinely, systematically, and intentionally prove outcomes. Thus, evidence-based measures of Student Affairs will become a more critical component to determining effectiveness of Student Affairs and services and impact on student success. Institutions that have yet to establish Student Affairs assessment must consider building capacity as a first step. During this stage, at a minimum, Student Affairs leaders must allocate adequate time to prepare and train staff for the process, secure buy-in, design initial measures, and analyze outcomes and provide continuous support.

References

Astin, A. W. (1993). *What matters in college? Four critical years revisited* (Vol. 1). San Francisco, CA: Jossey-Bass.

Beckhard, R. (1969). *Organizational development: Strategies and methods.* Reading, MA: Addison-Wesley.

Bentrim, E. M., & Henning, G. W. (2015). Tenet one: Building capacity in student affairs assessment. In K. Yousey- Elsener, E. M. Bentrim, & G. W. Henning (Eds.), *Coordinating student affairs divisional assessment: A practical guide* (pp. 1–10). Sterling, VA: Stylus Publishing.

Bresciani, M. J., Gardner, M. M., & Hickmott, J. (2009). *Demonstrating student success: A practical guide to outcomes- based assessment of learning and development in student affairs.* Sterling, VA: Stylus Publishing.

Duncan, A. G., & Holmes, R. H. (2015). Tenet three: Lay the foundation for a sustainable assessment culture. In R. P. Bingham, D. A. Bureau, & A. G. Duncan (Eds.), *Leading assessment for student success: Ten tenets that change culture and practice in student affairs* (pp. 41–50). Sterling, VA: Stylus Publishing.

Ewell, P. T. (2002). An emerging scholarship: A brief history of assessment. In T. W. Banta (Ed.), *Building a scholarship of assessment* (pp. 3–26). San Francisco, CA: Jossey-Bass.

Henning, G. W., & Roberts, D. (2016). *Student affairs assessment: Theory to practice.* Sterling, VA: Stylus Publishing.

Kuh, G. D. (2009). What student affairs professionals need to know about student engagement. *Journal of College Student Development, 50*(60), 683–709. doi:10.1353/csd.0.0099

Palomba, G. A., & Banta, T. W. (1999). *Assessment essentials: Planning, implementing and improving assessment in higher education.* San Francisco, CA: Jossey-Bass.

Pascarella, E. T., & Terenzini, P. T. (2005). *How college affects students: Findings and insights from twenty years of research.* San Francisco, CA: Jossey-Bass.

Schuh, J. H., & Gansemer-Topf, A. M. (2010). *The role of student affairs in student learning assessment* (NILOA Occasional Paper No. 7). Urbana, IL: University of Illinois and Indiana University, National Institute for Learning Outcomes Assessment. Retrieved from http://www.learningoutcomesassessment.org/documents/StudentAffairsRole.pdf

Whitt, E. J. (2005). *Promoting student success: What student affairs can do* (Occasional Paper No. 5). Bloomington, IN: Indiana University, Center for Postsecondary Research. Retrieved from http://nsse.indiana.edu/institute/documents/briefs/DEEP%20Practice%20Brief%205%20What%20Student%20Affairs%20Can%20Do.pdf

Yousey-Elsener, K., Bentrim, E. M., & Henning, G. W. (Eds.). (2015). *Coordinating student affairs divisional assessment: A practical guide.* Sterling, VA: Stylus Publishing.

3   Designing the Promise: The Salt Lake Community College Promise Program

Jason L. Taylor and Chuck W. Lepper

Introduction

The promise of the American Dream via an affordable public college education is under siege in the United States. A college degree has become a prerequisite to social and economic mobility, yet the price of college is increasingly out of reach to a majority of Americans. States have largely disinvested from public higher education (Mortensen, 2015); institutions have dramatically increased the price of tuition and fees (College Board, 2015); and federal financial aid has failed to address the complex needs of the lowest income students and families as the purchasing power of the Pell Grant has decreased over time (College Board, 2015).

Community colleges enroll nearly half of all undergraduate students in the United States, and they are the access point to higher education for millions of low-income students (American Association of Community Colleges [AACC], 2016). Average public community college tuition and fees for an in-district, full-time student is $3,435, almost a third less than the $9,410 for public four-year colleges and universities (College Board, 2015). Despite community colleges' commitment to access and affordability, the average cost of attendance for a full-time community college student is $16,833, and the average unmet need, after subtracting grant aid, is approximately $7,160 (College Board, 2015). This unmet need means that many low-income community college students must work or take out student loans while they are in college; in many cases, it means that they stop out of college. Research clearly shows that low-income students are more sensitive to prices and when faced with higher college prices, they are less likely to enroll in college than their more affluent peers (Castleman & Long, 2013; Long, 2004). Similarly, recent research shows that additional financial aid increases students' likelihood of being retained and completing college (Angrist, Autor, Hudson, & Pallais, 2015; Castleman & Long, 2013).

Within community colleges, Student Affairs divisions serve a critical student success function, including addressing students' financial and academic needs. One of the seven principles of good practice as outlined in ACPA/NASPA's *Principles of Good Practice in Student Affairs* is that Student Affairs should use resources effectively to help achieve institutional missions and goals (Blimling & Whitt, 1999). This principle suggests that Student Affairs divisions invest in and assess efforts that promote student learning and the goals of the institution. Given the increasing price of college for community college students and the large amount of unmet financial need, there is an opportunity for Student Affairs to play a larger role in addressing college affordability.

The purpose of this article is to describe the Salt Lake Community College (SLCC) Promise program, the role of Student Affairs in the design and implementation of SLCC Promise, and initial descriptive results of SLCC Promise program.

Addressing Student Needs: Promise Programs

The decline in college affordability has led to the proliferation of state and local financial aid programs and policies, often known as *promise* programs. Stimulated in part by President Obama's American College Promise in early 2015, *free college* and promise programs are expanding across the country. As of 2017, the College Promise Campaign estimated that there are approximately 190 existing programs, many of which were recently created (College Promise Campaign, 2015–2016). The purpose of many of these programs is simple: increase direct aid to students to increase affordability, access, and success. However, college student success is not solely determined by affordability, and existing promise programs may include additional design components that support students toward their goals such as encouraging or requiring service-related projects, academic advising, and full-time enrollment.

Although many promise programs are relatively new, research from long-standing programs such as Kalamazoo Promise and Pittsburgh Promise show that on average, these programs are having small, positive effects on students' access to and success in college (Andrews, DesJardins, & Ranchhod, 2010; Bartik, Hershbein, & Lachowska, 2015; Miller-Adams & Timmeney, 2013; Miron, Jones, & Kelaher-Young, 2012). Given the variation in promise program models and design, research has not determined which models are most effective and why.

SLCC and the SLCC Promise Program

SLCC is Utah's only comprehensive community college with an annual enrollment of approximately 60,000 students in credit and noncredit programs at one of its ten locations throughout Salt Lake County (SLCC, 2017a). The median age of students attending the college is 23 years old and the student population is approximately 68% White non-Hispanics, 17% Hispanic, 4% Asian, 2% Black, 1% Pacific Islander, and 1% Native American (SLCC, 2017b). The annual estimated cost of attendance is $3,528 for full-time students taking 12 credit hours or more per semester with approximately 18,000 students receiving financial aid during the 2015–2016 academic year (SLCC, 2017b). SLCC is accredited by the Northwest Commission on Colleges and Schools and offers a variety of associate's degree programs, certificates, and credentials. During the 2015–2016 academic year, SLCC was recognized as being the 12th highest producer of associate's degrees in the country among community colleges (SLCC, 2017b).

SLCC Promise Background

In 2016, SLCC's Board of Trustees endorsed a seven-year strategic plan. The goals of the strategic plan were to "increase student completion; improve transfer preparation and pathways; align with and respond to workforce needs; achieve equity in student participation and completion" and "secure institutional sustainability and capacity" (SLCC, 2016, p. 2). Through a collaborative process designed to support the strategic plan, the Division of Student Affairs (DOSA) proposed a tuition gap funding program, which would later become known as SLCC Promise.

The SLCC Promise is possible because of a state policy that allows institutions to waive tuition for some students. The Utah System of Higher Education's (USHE) Board of Regents (BOR) policy permits each USHE institution president to establish processes that grant individual students' full or partial tuition waivers. However, the policy stipulates that the amount of the waived tuition should not exceed more than 10% of the institution's anticipated total amount of tuition to be collected during a single fiscal year. Historically, SLCC utilized its allocation of tuition waivers to support student retention efforts by granting partial or full tuition waivers to students who served in leadership positions across the college and to allow academic departments to recruit and retain students in their academic programs. The amount of the tuition waivers was applied to the student's account before any financial aid or scholarship funds, frequently resulting in a significant tuition refund to the student, a first-dollar model. During the 2015–2016 academic year and prior to SLCC Promise, 581 SLCC students received either a partial or full tuition waiver.

SLCC Promise Design and Implementation

After reviewing the process by which tuition waivers were awarded and scanning the environment to leverage resources to support SLCC's strategic plan, DOSA developed the initial SLCC Promise design and submitted it to the college's president and executive cabinet for approval. The approved SLCC Promise initiative called for the use of the college's tuition waivers to provide gap funding for federal Pell Grant recipients, a last-dollar model. In order to maximize the use of tuition waivers allowed under the BOR policy, the process of applying the tuition waivers to student accounts was reengineered to apply any financial aid or scholarship funds first and fund any remaining balance with a partial tuition waiver to cover the full cost of tuition. Prior to implementation of the SLCC Promise, the college lacked a comprehensive strategy for disbursing tuition waivers and, as a result, lacked understanding of the tuition waivers' impact on student access and completion. Although SLCC Promise provides a more strategic use of resources, the tuition waiver disbursement change from first-dollar to last-dollar has resulted in significantly fewer students receiving refund balances from their Pell Grant or other forms of financial assistance. However, this change allowed SLCC to distribute the limited amount of tuition waivers to significantly more students, nearly doubling the number from 581 students in 2015–2016 to 1,059 in 2016–2017. Further, prior to SLCC Promise, financial need was not a strategic factor in the disbursement of waiver dollars, and SLCC Promise has shifted these dollars exclusively to low-income students who arguably have the most unmet need.

The SLCC Promise program includes four primary eligibility criteria and students must (a) complete the Free Application For Student Aid (FAFSA) and be eligible to receive a Pell Grant of any amount less than the cost of tuition; (b) register for a minimum of 12 credit hours; (c) meet with an academic advisor during their first semester of attendance and develop an academic plan that creates a clear pathway to degree or credential completion; and (d) maintain a minimum 2.0 grade point average.

The DOSA led the development and implementation of SLCC Promise, and DOSA's goal was to keep the process simple to increase accessibility of awards to students and to deliberately encourage students' successful completion of their degree goals. Student Affairs administrators believed that requiring recipients to complete an academic plan in conjunction with an academic advisor was critical to the individual's academic success and completion or transfer to a four-year institution. To simplify the process with continued focus on student success, SLCC determines eligibility based on the above criteria and e-mails students an auto-generated award notification with an electronic acceptance form. The electronic acceptance form provides general information about SLCC Promise, informs the students of the award requirements, and directs the student to schedule an appointment with an academic advisor to develop an academic plan for completion.

Once the student meets with the academic advisor, their complete academic plan is uploaded into the college's degree audit system and the completion of the academic plan is also noted in the college's student information system. The Office of Financial Aid verifies that students who have accepted an SLCC Promise award have completed academic plans within the degree audit system. After the verification has been completed and after the end of the college's drop and add period, the Office of Financial Aid applies the appropriate tuition waiver amount to the student's account.

It is important to note that SLCC Promise may only be used during the fall and spring semesters and may not be used during the summer term due to the unavailability of the federal Pell Grant, although this may change given recent changes to Pell availability in the summer terms. Additionally, SLCC Promise only covers tuition at the institution and does not cover general student fees or other costs of attendance. The SLCC Promise may be used to cover tuition costs up to 150% of the academic program's requirements. Finally, SLCC offers a number of noncredit competency-based programs and in compliance with the BOR policy, tuition waivers may not be applied to those programs, thus students enrolled in noncredit programs are not eligible to receive the SLCC Promise award.

Beyond Aid: Leveraging Student Affairs in Promise Programs

Beyond providing more aid to Pell Grant students, SLCC Promise has prompted new initiatives and collaborations that illustrate the significance of community college Student Affairs divisions in college access and success. For example, SLCC Promise has facilitated collaboration across the college and with the greater Salt Lake City community. Utah has one of the lowest FAFSA completion rates in the nation; only 30% of the state's resident students who attend higher education complete the FAFSA (USHE, 2016). In an effort to change this culture, in the spring of 2016, SLCC implemented a college funding initiative located at a site that serves a community with disproportionately high financial need. College funding advisors meet with prospective students and their family member to educate them about the financial aid process, available scholarships, and SLCC Promise and also assist them with completion of online FAFSA. During the 2016–2017 academic year, the college funding advisors met with 1,532 students and their family member, which resulted in 675 completed FAFSAs.

Additionally, SLCC Promise has helped forge stronger relationships between various departments and across divisional areas. For example, SLCC Promise requires more communication and collaboration within DOSA departments, and members of the Vice President for Student Affair's leadership team meet on a regular basis with representatives from the Office of Admissions, Office of Financial Aid, Office of Career and Academic Advising, and the Office of Marketing and Institutional Communication to continually coordinate SLCC Promise and to strategically plan future growth and development.

Finally, SLCC has been intentional in further developing relationships and communication with high school principals and high school guidance counselors within the SLCC service area. SLCC hosts an annual high school principals' luncheon and provides information regarding the performance of the high school's graduates at the college. The data shared with each principal include information on college readiness, first semester grade point averages, fall-to-spring persistence, fall-to-fall retention, demographics, and enrollment trends. SLCC also hosts an annual high school guidance counselor conference where similar information is presented, as well as providing tours and information about SLCC's ten campuses. In both cases, DOSA leverages these events to discuss and promote SLCC Promise and seek the assistance of high school principals and guidance counselors in promoting SLCC Promise.

Understanding SLCC Promise Participation and Descriptive Outcomes

As SLCC implements SLCC Promise, the college is dedicated to evaluating and studying SLCC Promise to understand who is benefiting from the program and its impact. Researchers have designed a multiple methods study to examine several research questions that examine who participates in SLCC Promise, the experiences of SLCC Promise participants, and the impact of SLCC Promise on students and on institutional outcomes. This article presents initial results from the fall 2016 cohort of students and answers the following research questions:

a   What are the characteristics of SLCC Promise participants?
b   Is there a difference in the characteristics of SLCC Promise students and all Pell Grant students?
c   Is there a difference in GPA and first-semester retention between SLCC Promise students and all Pell Grant students?

To answer the questions, the authors used institutional administrative data. The data include demographic variables (race/ethnicity, gender, age), enrollment information in AY2016–2017, and financial aid information. The authors restricted the sample only to those students who were Pell Grant recipients and enrolled at SLCC in fall 2016 ($n = 6{,}777$). Of these students, 534 received an SLCC Promise scholarship and the remaining 6,243 did not. The average amount of aid awarded to SLCC Promise recipients was $761 and the median was $762. To answer the research questions, the authors ran chi-square tests and t-tests to examine if there were statistically significant differences between Promise and non-Promise students.

Results

Table 3.1 presents the results to the first and second research questions. The average age of SLCC Promise recipients was 24, and a larger proportion of SLCC Promise recipients were female than male. Approximately 36% of SLCC Promise recipients were students of color. When compared to Pell Grant students who were non-Promise recipients, there was a statistically significant difference based on age and race/ethnicity. The average age of Promise recipients was 24 and the average age of non-Promise recipients was 26. Similarly, students of color represented a smaller share of Promise recipients compared to non-Promise recipients.

To answer the second research question, the authors restricted the sample to Pell Grant recipients who were first-time students in fall 2016 ($n = 2{,}504$) because the authors wanted to understand how receiving SLCC Promise related to the outcomes of students during their first semester at SLCC. The 2,504 first-time Pell Grant

Table 3.1 Characteristics of Pell Grant recipients in fall 2016, by promise and non-promise recipients

Student characteristic	Promise recipients (n = 534)	Non-promise recipients (n = 6,243)	Chi-square or t-test p-value
Age (mean)	24	26	<.001
Gender			.21
Male	45%	42%	
Female	55%	58%	
Race/Ethnicity			
Black	2%	4%	
Asian	6%	6%	
White	64%	60%	
Hispanic/Latinx	22%	23%	
Two or more races	4%	3%	
Pacific Islander	2%	2%	
Native American	1%	1%	
Nonresident	–	<1%	
Unknown	1%	<1%	
Binary race/ethnicity			<.01
Students of color	36%	40%	
White	64%	60%	

recipients represented 37% of all Pell Grant recipients enrolled in SLCC in fall 2016. Of the first-time students in fall 2016 who were Pell Grant recipients, 217 (9%) were Promise students. In order to compare outcomes of Promise students to more similar Pell Grant students, the authors further restricted the sample to students who were enrolled full time in fall 2016 because only full-time students are eligible for SLCC Promise. This resulted in 1,434 students; 1,217 of which did not receive Promise and 217 did receive Promise in fall 2016. Table 3.2 displays the results to the second research question that compares the demographic characteristics of these two groups. The results show that there were no statistically significant differences in demographics between the two groups; however, a slightly larger percentage of white students were Promise recipients ($p < .10$).

However, there were some interesting differences in outcomes between Promise and non-Promise recipients. First, Promise students had a statistically significant higher first-semester GPA (2.77)

Table 3.2 Characteristics and outcomes of full-time, first-time Pell Grant recipients in fall 2016, by promise and non-promise recipients

Student characteristic	Promise recipients (n = 217)	Non-promise recipients (n = 1,217)	Chi-square or t-test p-value
Age (mean)	23	23	.38
Gender			.30
Male	43%	47%	
Female	57%	53%	
Race/Ethnicity			
Black	<1%	6%	
Asian	7%	6%	
White	58%	52%	
Hispanic/Latinx	26%	29%	
Two or more races	5%	4%	
Pacific Islander	3%	3%	
Native American	1%	1%	
Nonresident	–	<1%	
Unknown	–	–	
Binary race/ethnicity			.09
Students of color	42%	49%	
White	58%	51%	
Fall 2016 GPA	2.77	2.48	<.01
Retention to spring 2017	82%	81%	.94
Number of credits enrolled, spring 17	12.70	12.24	<.05

compared to non-Promise students (2.48). Second, there was not a statistically significant difference in fall-to-spring retention between the two groups. However, Promise students were enrolled in significantly more credits than non-Promise Pell students in spring 2017.

Discussion

Nearly 200 colleges and universities have adopted free college and promise programs, and most recently, the State University System of New York and City University System of New York launched their new version of free college called the Excelsior Scholarship (SUNY, 2017). As free college and Promise programs expand in community colleges around the country, there is a need to understand the design of these programs, their outcomes, and the critical role of Student Affairs in distributing aid to students. Recognizing the increasing financial and academic needs of low-income students and the inefficient use of institutional aid dollars, DOSA led the conceptualization, design, and implementation of SLCC Promise. With DOSA's leadership, the institutional aid model at SLCC has shifted dramatically. Under the old model, institutional aid dollars were distributed in a way that was not aligned with SLCC's strategic vision, impacted a limited number of students, and did not explicitly consider students' need. Under the new SLCC Promise model, the limited institutional aid reaches a larger number of students, aligns with the strategic goals of supporting low-income students' success financially and academically, and more directly targets students with the greater financial need.

Among grant aid distributed at public institutions, public community colleges award the smallest share of institutional aid. For example, only 7% of grant aid awarded at public community colleges came from institutional aid, whereas institutional aid accounted for 53% of grant aid at public doctoral institutions, 33% at public master's, and 28% at public bachelor's (College Board, 2016). Research on need-based aid and merit-based aid has predominantly been limited to four-year institutions (e.g., DesJardins, Ahlburg, & McCall, 2002; Gross, Hossler, & Ziskin, 2007), but the recent proliferation of promise programs at community colleges raises interesting questions about how community colleges use institutional aid and how they consider need in the disbursement of their aid. Because many institution-based promise programs are so new, it is unclear the extent to which programs rely on institutional revenue sources for promise aid and how many have a need-based component. Many free college programs such as the new Excelsior Scholarship in New York and Tennessee Promise program have been criticized because aid eligibility is need-blind and being distributed to many students who do not have financial needs (Pingel, Parker, & Sisneros, 2016).

Similar to the development and launch of SLCC Promise, Student Affairs and Student Services can and should play an important role in the design of free community college programs. First, they can advocate that institutional aid be directed to more students with unmet financial need in order to increase their access to and success in college. Even though community colleges have fewer resources and distribute less aid than other public higher education sectors, directing scarce resources to students who most need it can support low-income students' retention and success and align with strategic institutional priorities. The early evidence presented in this manuscript show that SLCC Promise recipients have a higher first-semester GPA and enroll in a slightly larger credit load in the semesters than other full-time Pell recipients who did not receive Promise. Although these relationships are not causal and additional research is needed, this evidence is promising about the potential of the SLCC Promise program. Second, Student Affairs can help design free college programs and policies so that they integrate other support services like academic advising. Despite evidence that suggests additional financial assistance can support student outcomes (Angrist et al., 2015; Castleman & Long, 2013), research also suggests that when financial aid is coupled with more comprehensive support services, low-income students are even more successful (Clotfelter, Hemelt, & Ladd, 2017). Finally, Student Affairs should consider the potential unintended consequences of free college programs as they design them. For example, many programs have eligibility requirements that students attend full-time or that they enroll in college immediately after high school (Kelchen, 2017). Although arguably well-intended and aligned with institutional goals to increase college enrollment and support timely completion, these types of eligibility requirements shut out many students that the community college serves and limit free college programs to a more traditional student population. Student Affairs can help the institution think creatively about how to construct eligibility requirements in a fair and equitable way.

Acknowledgments

The authors would like to acknowledge the faculty and staff at SLCC who have worked hard to develop and implement SLCC Promise and the students for whom SLCC Promise supports. The authors also want to acknowledge the SLCC Institutional Research Director, Jeff Webb, and Assistant Director, Rochelle Smits, for supporting data collection on SLCC Promise.

References

American Association of Community Colleges. (2016). *Fast facts from our fact sheet.* Retrieved from http://www.aacc. nche.edu/AboutCC/Pages/fastfactsfactsheet.aspx

Andrews, R., DesJardins, S., & Ranchhod, V. (2010). The effects of the Kalamazoo Promise on college choice. *Economics of Education Review, 29,* 722–737.

Angrist, J., Autor, D., Hudson, S., & Pallais, A. (2015). Evaluating econometric evaluation of post-secondary aid. *American Economic Review, 105*(5), 502–507.

Bartik, T., Hershbein, B., & Lachowska, M. (2015, February). Longer-term effects of the Kalamazoo Promise Scholarship on college enrollment, persistence, and completion. In *American Education Finance and Policy Annual Conference*, Washington, DC.

Blimling, G. S., & Whitt, E. J. (1999). *Good practice in student affairs: Principles to foster student leadership*. San Francisco, CA: Jossey-Bass.

Castleman, B. L., & Long, B. T. (2013). *Looking beyond enrollment: The causal effect of need-based grants on college access, persistence, and graduation*. NBER working paper no. 19306. Cambridge, MA: National Bureau of Economic Research.

Clotfelter, C. T., Hemelt, S. W., & Ladd, H. F. (2017). Multifaceted aid for low-income students and college outcomes: Evidence from North Carolina. *Economic Inquiry, 56*, 278–303. doi:10.1111/ecin.12486

College Board. (2015). *Trends in college pricing 2015*. New York, NY: Author.

College Board. (2016). *Trends in student aid 2016*. New York, NY: Author.

College Promise Campaign. (2015–2016). *Annual report: College Promise Campaign*. Washington, DC: Author.

DesJardins, S. L., Ahlburg, D. A., & McCall, B. P. (2002). Simulating the longitudinal effects of changes in financial aid on student departure from college. *Journal of Human Resources, 37*, 653–679.

Gross, J. P. K., Hossler, D., & Ziskin, M. (2007). Institutional aid and student persistence: An analysis of the effects of institutional financial aid at public four-year institutions. *NASFAA Journal of Student Financial Aid, 37*(1), 28–39.

Kelchen, R. (2017, July). *A review of college promise programs: Evidence from the Midwest*. Minneapolis, MN: Midwestern Higher Education Compact.

Long, B. T. (2004). How have college decisions changed over time? An application of the conditional logistic choice model. *Journal of Econometrics, 121*, 271–296.

Miller-Adams, M., & Timmeney, B. (2013). *The impact of the Kalamazoo Promise on college choice: An analysis of Kalamazoo area math and science center graduates*. Kalamazoo, MI: W.E. Upjohn Institute of Employment Research.

Miron, G., Jones, J., & Kelaher-Young, A. (2012). The impact of the Kalamazoo Promise on student attitudes, goals, and aspirations. *American Secondary Education, 40*(2), 5–27.

Mortensen, T. (2015). *State investment and disinvestment in higher education, 1969–2015*. Washington, DC: Pell Institute for the Study of Opportunity in Higher Education.

Pingel, S., Parker, E., & Sisneros, L. (2016). *Free community college: An approach to increase adult student success in postsecondary education*. Boulder, CO: Education Commission of the States.

SLCC. (2016). *Your community college: SLCC strategic plan 2016–2023.* Salt Lake City, UT: Author. Retrieved from http://performance.slcc.edu/Strategic_Plan/Strategic%20Planning%202016.pdf

SLCC. (2017a). *About SLCC.* Retrieved from http://www.slcc.edu/about/index.aspx

SLCC. (2017b). *Fact books.* Retrieved from https://www.slcc.edu/about/fact-book.aspx

SUNY. (2017). The Excelsior Scholarship is leading the way to college affordability. Retrieved from http://www.suny.edu/smarttrack/types-of-financial-aid/scholarships/excelsior/

USHE. (2016). *FAFSA completions up in Utah, down nationwide.* Retrieved from https://higheredutah.org/fafsa-completions-up-in-utah-down-nationwide/

4 Collaborative Impact and Professional Development: Effective Student Services for Immigrant Populations Amid Growing Inequality

William Watson, Adela Esquivel-Swinson, and Roland Montemayor

San José, California, is the largest city in Silicon Valley and the tenth largest city in the United States. San José represents a tale of two cities where the immense wealth and vitality of the technology sector has not transferred to the social sector sufficiently to mitigate inequality (Johnson, 2015). The abundance which has accrued to some has left others marginalized, realizing little gain from a growing economy (Bohn & Danielson, 2016). This status quo forecasts compromised competitiveness due to shortages of skilled labor. Importing talent is not sustainable and shipping jobs to other markets further marginalizes opportunity for the increasingly diverse population (Treuhaft, Blackwell, & Pastor, 2011).

The San José Evergreen Community College District (SJECCD) plays a central role in the regional educational ecosystem where 182,645 people over 18 years of age do not have the equivalent of a high school diploma and an estimated 70,000 people of 18–34 years of age are undocumented (Messaro, 2017; U.S. Census Bureau, 2015). The growing immigrant population, including undocumented students and their families, relies on an education system statewide which now structures alignment between the California Department of Education—Adult Education (*English as a Second Language, English Language—Civics, Adult Secondary Education, and Career and Technical Education*) and the statewide system of 113 community colleges through Adult Education Community College consortia (Adult Education Block Grant [AEBG], 2017).

The San José Evergreen Community College District embraces this state-level system change to grow its capacity and increase opportunity for both immigrant and low-income populations. A two-pronged strategy for building the capacity of the SJECCD to strengthen services to both immigrant and low-income populations outlined here uses required and optional collaborative change initiatives coupled with professional development for student services personnel. Building capacity for effective student services amid growing inequality strengthens institutional effectiveness, promotes economic mobility, and prepares a highly skilled workforce for a globally competitive Silicon Valley (Reidenbach, 2016).

Mandated and Chosen Collaborative Change Initiatives

Mandated System-Level Change (71 Adult Education—College Consortia Statewide)

California community colleges are the open access portal to higher education opportunity. However, thousands of Californians for whom college is out of reach include a disproportionate number of immigrants, English language learners, low-income families, and adults with less than a High School diploma—precisely those served by Adult Education in California (Montes & Choitz, 2016). Mitigating barriers to Adult School access and then creating structural alignments between Adult Schools and community colleges are essential components to preparing a highly skilled workforce that reflects the diversity of California (Conway & Dawson, 2016).

Representing a significant change in the California education ecosystem, The California Community Colleges Chancellor's Office and the California Department of Education now jointly administer Adult Education through established consortia that partner adult schools with their region's community colleges (Adult Education Block Grant [AEBG], 2017). Seventy-one such consortia now exist in California. The consortium served by SJECCD is The South Bay Consortium for Adult Education (SBCAE), a collaboration of four colleges from two community college districts, and five adult schools in Santa Clara County, California, designed to implement a regional plan to expand and improve the delivery of adult education. Key SBCAE features include (a) integrated no wrong door student-centered education and services, (b) contextualized pathways to promising careers, (c) mitigating income inequality promoting economic self-sufficiency, and (d) immigrant integration (SBCAE, 2017a).

The work of the SBCAE Consortium triggers institutional change throughout the SJECCD, which has historically offered few noncredit courses. Creating the capacity to offer noncredit programs benefits a previously underserved population who enroll in open entry courses in contextualized career pathways, which do not incur fees and therefore do not deplete financial aid while completing developmental education, conserving resources required for degree attainment (Callahan & Perna, 2015). In addition to these structural changes, the SBCAE employs Transition Support Specialists who work directly with adult learners to navigate systems and persist toward achieving their educational goals. The time and effort otherwise spent learning systems navigation no longer takes away from learning in the classroom. College faculty develop contextualized noncredit career pathways for adult learners to earn credentials and achieve economic self-sufficiency. Pathways are designed by faculty and undergo the institutional curriculum approval process. Pathways developed to date include Engineering Careers, Medical Careers, Surveying—Geomatics, Automotive Technology, and Pre-Apprenticeship (SBCAE, 2017b).

Optional Collaborative Change Initiatives Chosen to Add Value (SparkPoint and ALLIES)

Collaborative partnerships strengthen institutional outcomes (Eddy, 2010; Kezar & Lester, 2009; Scearce, 2016, StriveTogether, 2016). To further strengthen retention, the SBCAE is collaborating with United Way Bay Area to implement SparkPoint San José. SparkPoint Centers employ financial coaches who support students and others to bundle financial capability services and resources to increase income, improve credit, access available benefits and other resources, and build savings. SparkPoint is not restricted to students. Financial coaches work with community members who are not enrolled but could enroll if their financial circumstances were stabilized. SparkPoint represents an optional change initiative embedded within SBCAE that will grow to serve students throughout San José. To deliver the full range of financial capability services envisioned in the SparkPoint model, colleges must collaborate with multiple organizations to provide services not typically offered in a college setting such as matched savings accounts, credit repair, safe financial products, public benefits, housing supports, legal services, tax preparation assistance, and food security (United Way Bay Area [UWBA], 2017). The efficacy of SparkPoint in community colleges has shown striking results. The first SparkPoint in a California community college was launched in 2010 at Skyline College in

San Bruno, California. The fall to spring academic persistence rate for students who participated in one SparkPoint service is on average an 81% academic persistence rate. Students who participated in two or more services had on average a 93% academic persistence rate (Skyline College, 2016). SparkPoint San José will be a new center in the regional UWBA SparkPoint Initiative, which uses a customized data system to measure incremental gains in economic mobility uniformly across the San Francisco Bay Area SparkPoint Centers.

SBCAE partners with the Alliance for Language Learners' Integration, Education, and Success (ALLIES) to extend its competencies in immigrant integration. A design team has been working since 2016 with funding from the Silicon Valley Community Foundation to build an Immigrant Integration Framework. The Framework is the subject of a policy paper, available on the ALLIES website, which defines eight goal areas and metrics including economic security, English proficiency, credentials and residency, health and well-being, educational and career advancement, first language literacy, providing for children and family, and participation in civic and community life (ALLIES, 2017).

The framework works equally to not only function as a menu with metrics to inventory immigrant needs but also immigrant contributions. Multiple service providers can also use the tool to assess organizational effectiveness in serving immigrant communities and determine community-level mapping of resources (ALLIES, 2017). The SBCAE–ALLIES partnership was honored with the 2017 Beacon of Light Award from the Santa Clara County Office of Immigrant Relations for work to improve the lives of immigrants and refugees (Santa Clara County, 2017).

Student Services Academy for all Student Services Personnel in the SJECCD

SJECCD Human Resources collaborated with the SJECCD campus Vice President of Student Affairs from each college and the SJECCD Workforce Institute to custom design a yearlong recurring Student Services Academy that provides the student services staff three training sessions throughout the year. Curriculum was tailored in response to an assessment of need and the delivery was structured as an enjoyable but mandatory experience. The Student Services Academy learnings will be incorporated in the employee evaluation process. Topics at the kickoff retreat included the following: (a) What Student Services Excellence Means; (b) Threats to Service Excellence; (c) How to Build Rapport with Students and Build Trust; (d) Dealing with Stressful Situations; (e) Equity, Diversity and Inclusion; and (f) Effective Responses to Oppression.

The Student Services Academy signals a significant institutional investment in staff, sets expectations for service norms, and fosters team building that is rooted in a process of growth to enhance organizational capacity. The investment will produce a group of staff in student services who are culturally responsive to the influx of previously underserved populations newly generated by collaborative impact initiatives. Over 80% of Student Services Academy Retreat participants surveyed ranked the quality of presenters four or higher with five being the highest quality (SJECCD Human Services, 2017).

Implications for Community College Practice, Policy, and Research

- Engaging collaborative initiatives that include diverse organizations external to typical college operations triggers change within the college that would otherwise be either difficult to imagine or difficult to achieve without the external initiative (Kezar & Lester, 2009). For example, SparkPoint implementation depends on mitigating the organizational silos across internal programs and departments as well as engaging multiple partner organizations each with diverse requirements for effective interface. Both internal and external relations depend on a highly agile student-centered service orientation, which differs from program- or institution-centered orientations.
- Increasing the reach of the college into underserved communities demands capacity building for programmatic and curricular innovations. It also demands a proportional investment in staff development to ensure proficiency in service delivery equal to the demand.
- Complex collaboration can be obstructed by status-quo change resistors who unwittingly or intentionally derail capacity-building fearing a perceived loss of power and autonomy, or distrusting others outside their lines of authority. Change is hard even if change forecasts the viability and relevance of an organization into the future (Eddy, 2010).
- Each organization in collaborative efforts must reflect on and mitigate biases that perpetuate systems of privilege and oppression including racism, patriarchy, classism, intellectual elitism, heterosexism, and ethnocentrism (Wolff et al., 2017).

References

Adult Education Block Grant [AEBG]. (2017). *Adult education block grant: History of AB 86 and the planning process.* Retrieved from http://aebg. cccco.edu/About/AB-86-Planning

ALLIES. (2017). *Immigrant integration framework: From English learning to full participation.* Alliance for Language Learners' Integration, Education and Success. Retrieved from: http://www.allies4innovation.org/our-work/iip/

Bohn, S., & Danielson, C. (2016). *Income inequality and the safety net in California.* Public Policy Institute of California. Retrieved from http://www.ppic.org/content/pubs/report/R_516SBR.pdf

Callahan, M., & Perna, L. (2015). *Indicators of higher education equity in the United States: A 45 year trend report.* Pell Institute for the Study of Opportunity in Higher Education. Retrieved from http://www.pellinstitute.org/downloads/ publications-Indicators_of_Higher_Education_Equity_in_the_US_45_Year_Trend_Report.pdf

Conway, M., & Dawson, S. L. (2016). *Restore the promise work: Reducing inequality by raising the floor and building ladders.* Washington, DC: Aspen Institute. Retrieved from https://www.aspeninstitute.org/publications/restore-the-promise-of-work-reducinginequality-by-raising-the-floor-and-building-ladders/

Eddy, P. (2010). *Partnerships and collaborations in higher education: ASHE* (Vol. 36, p. 2). San Francisco, CA: Jossey-Bass.

Johnson, J. (2015). *San José Mayor: Boom has created A Tale of Two Cities.* Joshua Johnson Interview with San Jose Mayor Sam Liccardo for KQED News. San Francisco. Retrieved from https://ww2.kqed.org/news/2015/01/28/san-jose-mayor-boom-has-created-atale-of-two-cities/

Kezar, A. J., & Lester, J. (2009). *Organizing higher education for collaboration: A guide for campus leaders.* San Francisco, CA: Jossey-Bass.

Messaro, R. (2017). *2017 Silicon Valley index. Institute for regional studies.* Joint Venture Silicon Valley. Retrieved from https://www.jointventure.org/images/stories/pdf/index2017.pdf

Montes, M. A., & Choitz, V. (2016). *Improving immigrant access to workforce services: Partnerships, practices & policies.* Washington, DC: Workforce Strategies Initiative of the Aspen Institute. Retrieved from https://www.aspeninstitute.org/publications/improvingimmigrant-access-workforce-services-partnerships-practices-policies/

Reidenbach, L. (2016). *Inequality and economic security in Silicon Valley.* California Budget & Policy Center. Retrieved from http://calbudgetcenter.org/wp-content/uploads/Inequality-and-Economic-Security-in-Silicon-Valley-05.25.2016.pdf

San Jose Evergreen Community College District. (2017). *Equal employment opportunity & diversity plan.* Retrieved from http://www.sjeccd.edu/AdministrativeServices/Documents/EEO-DIVERSITY-PLAN_BOARD-ADOPTED2017MAY9-FINALVERSION_withSignature.pdf

Santa Clara County. (2017). *Beacon of light award. Office of immigrant relations.* Retrieved from https://www.sccgov.org/sites/oir

Scearce, D. (2016). *Catalyzing networks for social change: A funder's guide. Monitor Institute.* Washington, DC: Grantmakers for Effective Organizations. Retrieved from http://www.monitorinstitute.com/downloads/what-we-think/catalyzingnetworks/Catalyzing_Networks_for_Social_Change.pdf

Skyline College. (2016). *SparkPoint program review.* Retrieved from https://skylinecollege.edu/comprehensiveprogramreview/assets/programreview_april2016/sparkpoint.pdf

South Bay Consortium for Adult Education [SBCAE]. (2017a). *Serving over 30,000 adult education students in Santa Clara County.* Retrieved from http://sbcae.org/ab86-ab104/

South Bay Consortium for Adult Education. (2017b). *Three year regional plan.* Retrieved October 9, 2016, from http://sbcae.org/regional-plan/

StriveTogether. (2016). *Creating strive together cradle to career network.* Retrieved from http://www.strivetogether.org/cradle-career-network

Treuhaft, S., Blackwell, A. G., & Pastor, M. (2011). *America's tomorrow: Equity is the superior growth model.* PolicyLink and USC's Program for Environmental and Regional Equity. Retrieved from http://www.policylink.org/sites/default/files/SUMMIT_FRAMING_WEB_20120110.PDF

U.S. Census Bureau. (2015). *2011–2015 American Community Survey 5-year estimates.* Table B15001: SEX BY AGE BY EDUCATIONAL ATTAINMENT FOR THE POPULATION 18 YEARS AND OVER; Generated by Shusaku Horibe; using American Fact Finder. Retrieved March 17, 2017, from https://factfinder.census.gov/faces/tableservices/jsf/pages/productview.xhtml?pid=ACS_15_5YR_B15001&prodType=table

United Way Bay Area. (2017). *SparkPoint.* Retrieved from https://uwba.org/SparkPoint

Wolff, T., Minkler, M., Wolfe, S., Berkowitz, B., Bowen, L., Butterfoss, F. D., … Lee, K. S. (2017). *Collaborating for equity and justice: Moving beyond collective impact.* Nonprofit Quarterly. Winter 2016. Retrieved from https://nonprofitquarterly.org/2017/01/09/collaborating-equity-justice-moving-beyond-collective-impact/

5 Exploring the Availability and Influence of LGBTQ+ Student Services Resources on Student Success at Community Colleges: A Mixed Methods Analysis

David J. Nguyen, G. Blue Brazelton, Kristen A. Renn, and Michael R. Woodford

Two-year institutions comprise a large sector of postsecondary education, enrolling approximately 41% of undergraduate students in the United States (American Association of Community Colleges, 2017). These institutions have long provided educational opportunities for underserved student populations, by removing many of the barriers to admission, such as standardized testing and high cost of tuition (Meier, 2013). Even though two-year institutions provide an avenue for educational attainment for diverse and underrepresented student populations, these institutions are sensitive to economic variations in federal and state appropriations that can affect how resources, including student services, are distributed (Dowd & Cheslock, 2006; Goldrick-Rab, 2010; Katsinas & Tollefson, 2009). Previous research has identified a positive relationship between the availability of resources and academic success (Bound, Lovenheim, & Turner, 2009), and competition among academic and nonacademic units for fungible resources (e.g., monetary, campus spaces, administrative support) on a campus may limit students' ability to reach their academic potential. Nonacademic units, such as student services, ask for these resources to support co-curricular opportunities, mental health resources, career development, and advocacy reasons.

Students attending two-year institutions often come from historically marginalized groups, including the lesbian, gay, bisexual, transgender, and queer (LGBTQ+) community. Scholars have investigated how students with varying social identities (e.g., race/ethnicity, ability, first generation) experience two-year institutions (Calcagno, Bailey, Jenkins, Kienzl, & Leinbach, 2008; Greene, Marti & McClenney, 2008). While this research has been helpful to furthering knowledge of various student populations, LGBTQ+ students have received sparse attention (Ivory, 2005; Sanlo, 2012; Sanlo & Espinoza, 2012; Zamani-Gallaher & Choudhuri, 2016). Numerous studies have demonstrated the negative relationship between LGBTQ+ students and campus climate at four-year institutions; however, few studies have considered the two-year institution context (Brown, Clarke, Gortmaker, & Robinson-Keilig, 2004; Garvey, Taylor, & Rankin, 2015; Ivory, 2005; Rankin, Blumenfeld, Weber, & Frazer, 2010; Woodford & Kulick, 2015). Until recently, so few studies focused on LGBTQ+ students attending two-year institutions that Ivory (2005) concluded "[d]ue to the invisible nature of the LGBTQ undergraduate population, it is difficult for Student Affairs professionals at community colleges to identify and address the needs of sexual minority students on campus" (p. 482). In short, Ivory (2005) pointed out that very little empirical evidence has been published on LGBTQ+ students attending two-year institutions. LGBTQ+ students are rendered invisible within large bodies of literature related to LGBTQ+ students and two-year institutions. Most research studies with LGBTQ+ student populations occur at research institutions. These studies have informed Student Affairs practitioners employed at this institutional type. While this growing body of literature documents how many LGBTQ+ students experience postsecondary education, these studies do not attend to the unique context two-year institutions fulfill. Garvey and colleagues (2015) suggested that the paucity of research concerning LGBTQ+ students at two-year institutions "leaves scholars and practitioners without empirical evidence to substantiate claims" regarding campus environments for sexually minoritized students (p. 528). This study highlights the need for identity-specific resources and their value in contributing to student success.

Many two- and four-year institutions provide resources to support students' academic and, in some cases, social outcomes. One way that institutions intercede is through the introduction of student support resources, but two-year institutions generally do not operate with the same complement of resources available at many four-year institutions. Compared to other institutional types, two-year institutions often have the fewest resources for students, especially for the most disadvantaged students (Bailey & Morest, 2006). Higher education scholars frequently acknowledge that student-centered resources (e.g., campus centers, identity-focused centers) and campus environments play an important role in student learning experiences, opportunities, and outcomes (Mayhew et al., 2016; Pascarella & Terenzini, 2005; Strange & Banning, 2015). The lack of these resources within two-year colleges may disrupt transfer pathways to four-year institutions, interrupt degree completion, or inhibit a student's ability to secure employment upon degree completion (Bailey & Alfonso, 2005; Karp, 2011).

Like other students holding marginalized identities, LGBTQ+ students often seek specific resources to contribute to their success and to counteract pervasively homophobic, heterosexist, and transphobic campus environments (Garvey et al., 2015; Taylor, Dockendorff, & Inselman, 2018). LGBTQ+ students attending community colleges are at varying stages of sexual identity development, "often seeking the services of Student Affairs professionals," and may require the assistance from student support services to advocate for equitable experiences (Leider, 2000, p. 3). Community college students may face unique challenges in their LGBTQ+ development compared to four-year institution peers. For example, unlike those attending four-year residential institutions, LGBTQ+ community college students frequently commute, which may "not permit the same kind of experimentation and exaggerated risks that a sheltered residential campus can provide" (Leck, 1998, p. 378). Without resources to aid this exploration, some college students may attempt to conceal their marginalized identity (Bieschke, Eberz, & Wilson, 2000), which can contribute to distress and other negative outcomes. Clearly, given their potential role in fostering students' success and healthy development, there is a need to examine the LGBTQ+-specific resources at community colleges.

Background

Campus climate research for LGBTQ+ student populations has identified higher education as being particular hostile, chilly, and discriminatory. Thus far, only one published study (Garvey et al., 2015) has specifically assessed the campus climate for LGBTQ students ($n = 102$) attending two-year institutions. Garvey et al. (2015) identified classroom spaces as being hostile and anti-LGBT. Negative classroom experiences correlated with negative perceptions of campus climate. Numerous participants reported that they considered leaving school because they did not feel supported. Garvey et al. (2015) concluded that a negative "relationship between students' campus experiences and desirable student outcomes suggests LGBTQ community college students' learning, development, and persistence may be at risk" (p. 537). A particular challenge facing two-year institutions is that the resources students need to succeed may be absent from campus (Beemyn, 2012; Ivory, 2005; Manning, Pring, & Glider, 2012; Zamani-Gallaher & Choudhuri, 2011).

While only a few studies have been published on LGBTQ+ students attending two-year institutions, scholarly attention has illuminated the needs and experiences of this student population (Beemyn, 2012; Leider, 2012; Sanlo & Espinoza, 2012; Zamani-Gallaher & Choudhuri, 2011). This research challenges the assumption that the experience of LGBTQ+ students at community colleges is similar to that of students attending four-year institutions (Leider, 2012). For example, Zamani-Gallaher and Choudhuri (2016) qualitatively explored the coming-out experiences, adequacy of student support services, and welcoming nature of campus climate with 11 LGBTQ students and seven staff at a community college. Study results illustrated students' interest in pursuing social connections outside classrooms, their feelings of being ignored inside curricular contexts, and their seeking of student resources to address personal challenges.

Turning to LGBTQ+ students themselves, some prospective two-year college students may use the Campus Pride Index to "decode" campus climate for LGBTQ+ students (Campus Pride Index, 2017; Taylor et al., 2018, p. 155). This index uses 50+ self-report questions to assess eight LGBTQ-friendly factors, including LGBTQ Policy Inclusion, LGBTQ Support and Institutional Commitment, LGBTQ Academic Life, LGBTQ Student Life, LGBTQ Housing, LGBTQ Campus Safety, LGBTQ Counseling and Health, and LGBTQ Recruitment and Retention Efforts. Out of the 274 participating institutions, 19 community or technical colleges participated in the assessment and listed their associated rating with the Campus Pride Index (2017). However, this low number should not be interpreted to mean that two-year institutions do not want to provide inclusive spaces for LGBTQ+ students. It is possible that individual campuses may not be aware of the web-based tool (Taylor et al., 2018) or participation may not be a priority or possibility, due to limited resources.

Concerning student services and resources at two-year institutions, considerable research exists, often centering on the connection between resources and student success, especially persistence (Bailey & Alfonso, 2005; Nitecki, 2011; Wood & Harris, 2013). Similar to what is found in the literature on student engagement at four-year institutions, students at two-year institutions are more likely to be academically successful if they use institutional resources (Crisp & Taggart, 2013). Supplementing this conclusion is that engaging with nonacademic resources can lead to positive student outcomes related to persistence and retention at two-year institutions (Karp, 2011).

In summary, previous studies have chronicled the negative experiences of LGBTQ+ students attending two-year institutions (Beemyn, 2012; Garvey et al., 2015; Ivory, 2005; Leider, 2000, 2012; Sanlo, 2012; Sanlo & Espinoza, 2012; Zamani-Gallaher & Choudhuri, 2011, 2016). These theoretical and empirical articles consistently document the absence of student support services for LGBTQ+ students (Beemyn, 2012; Garvey et al., 2015; Manning et al., 2012; Zamani-Gallaher & Choudhuri, 2016). What is clear from the extant literature is that researchers should explore the availability and demand for LGBTQ+ student support services at two-year institutions. This study specifically addresses this gap by exploring the availability of select LGBTQ+ resources and how they have benefitted LGBTQ+ students.

Theoretical Framework

This study focuses on how specific microsystems within Bronfenbrenner's (1993) ecological systems theory foster success for LGBTQ+ students through their experiences and interactions with various campus resources. Bronfenbrenner's (1979) ecological systems theory postulates that researchers studying human development need to move beyond "direct observation" of one or more individuals in the same place (p. 21). Instead, researchers should consider an "examination of multiperson systems of interaction not limited to a single setting and must take into account aspects of the environment beyond the immediate situation containing subject" (p. 21). Bronfenbrenner's (1993) theory involves interactions among four interrelated parts: person-process-context-time (PPCT). PPCT centers the individual (*person*) in a particular *context*. According to Bronfenbrenner (1979), person begins accounting for various influences of individuals. Process emphasizes the interactions and responses an individual has with their proximal and distal environments (*context*). Finally, time reflects the sequence and timing of life events and sociocultural shifts on an individual's development.

In this study, we focus upon how LGBTQ+ college students at two-year institutions experience success through campus resources. Students attending two-year institutions bring personal experiences and characteristics with them to campus. Experiences and characteristics include the student's identity characteristics (e.g., sexual orientation, gender identity, race/ethnicity, socioeconomic status), academic preparation, and high school environments (e.g., positive, negative). Individuals interact with people and resources in their environments. How the individual responds to these contexts evokes processes fostering human development. Individuals are nested within five layers of context; these contexts exert lessening degrees of influence on the individual as these influences move further away from the core. The first level is the microsystem. Microsystems reflect people, resources, or contexts that have direct influence on the individual. Most importantly, microsystems do not materialize in isolation. Many microsystems are present for a person and, in some cases, they link together to create mesosystems. Mesosystems may be best described as "linkages" between multiple contexts for the person. Exosystems appear when there is not a direct influence, instead an indirect influence on the developmental possibilities of the person is affected (Renn & Arnold, 2003). At the most distal position from the center, macrosystems exist and reflect different patterns of the previously described system characteristics. Beyond the macrosystem, the chronosystem reflects the final component, *time.* The chronosystem illustrates the development of the individual over time. More specifically, the chronosystem "is seen as embedded in and powerfully shaped by conditions and events occurring during the historical period through which the person lives" (Bronfenbrenner, 1995, p. 641).

The college experience cannot be isolated to a single microsystem. Multiple systems join and link together to create a "mesosystem" that affects the development and experience of the individual. Extracurricular activities, campus resources, student involvement, and classrooms serve as examples of on-campus microsystems (Renn & Arnold, 2003). Community college students are likely to have diverse off-campus microsystems including workplace, family, and community. The present application of Bronfenbrenner's explores how microsystems (e.g., LGBTQ+ counseling services, LGBTQ+ resource centers, Gay-Straight Alliance student organizations) support an LGBTQ+ student's success within the two-year campus environment.

Methods

Data used in this study are from the National Study of LGBTQ+ College Student Success (NSLGBTQSS; http://www.lgbtqsuccess.net). The present analysis utilized a concurrent mixed methods design, "which combines elements of qualitative and quantitative research approaches. . .for the purposes of breadth and depth of understanding and corroboration" (Johnson, Onwuegbuzie, & Turner, 2007, p. 123). This study's concurrent mixed methods research design combined an online survey instrument with semi-structured interviews. Together, the quantitative and qualitative tools addressed factors and influences on the support and success of LGBTQ+-identified college students.

Procedures

The analytic sample for this study represents a subset from the larger project exploring LGBTQ+ college student success. This analysis draws upon 936 survey responses from the NSLGBTQSS (two-year and four-year institutions represented) and 12 semi-structured interviews conducted with current and recent community college students. Before beginning data collection, the principal investigators applied for and received institutional review board approval for the study.

Quantitative Data, Variables, and Analyses

Participants ($N = 952$) were recruited at an LGBTQ+ and ally student conference or through LGBTQ listservs and networks. We reduced the quantitative analytic sample to 936 students who completed responses to LGBTQ+ resource-related questions. The survey contained demographic questions, academic outcomes, health outcomes, LGBTQ+ interpersonal protective and stress factors, and knowledge of resource availability at the individual's institution. Table 5.1 contains participant demographics.

In this paper, we report on the LGBTQ+-specific resources available at the campus the student attended, as reported by the student. Participant responses are grouped by institutional type (determined by highest degree granted) as follows: 49 associates only, 136 bachelor's only, 209 master's, and 542 doctoral-granting institutions. We explore whether or not students indicated if the following existed at their school: LGBTQ+ resource centers, LGBTQ+ counseling, LGBTQ+ career planning, and LGBTQ+ student organizations. To examine differences in LGBTQ+ resources across each type of institution, we conducted chi-square analysis.

Qualitative Data and Analyses

Sixty semi-structured interviews were conducted with purposefully selected participants, and for this paper we used interviews from

Table 5.1 Summary of participant demographics by institution type and overall (*N* = 936)

Demographic characteristic	Associates n (%)	Bachelor's n (%)	Master's n (%)	Doctoral n (%)	Overall n (%)
Assigned birth sex					
Female	18 (37)	42 (31)	65 (31)	222 (41)	347 (37)
Male	31 (63)	94 (69)	143 (68)	315 (58)	583 (62)
Missing	0 (0)	0 (0)	1 (0)	5 (1)	6 (1)
Primary gender identity					
Cisgender man	21 (43)	38 (28)	56 (27)	208 (38)	323 (35)
Cisgender woman	16 (33)	69 (51)	100 (48)	233 (43)	418 (45)
Genderqueer	3 (6)	18 (13)	27 (13)	50 (9)	98 (10)
Two-spirit	1 (2)	1 (1)	2 (1)	4 (1)	8 (1)
Transgender	6 (12)	5 (4)	13 (6)	29 (5)	53 (6)
Other identity	2 (4)	5 (4)	11 (5)	17 (3)	35 (4)
Missing	0 (0)	0 (0)	0 (0)	1 (0)	1 (0)
Primary sexual orientation					
Asexual	1 (2)	6 (4)	5 (2)	11 (2)	23 (2)
Bisexual	6 (12)	29 (21)	39 (19)	65 (12)	139 (15)
Gay	12 (24)	29 (21)	45 (22)	171 (32)	257 (27)
Heterosexual	3 (6)	1 (1)	8 (4)	12 (2)	24 (3)
Lesbian	8 (16)	23 (17)	34 (16)	92 (17)	157 (17)
Man-loving-man	0 (0)	0 (0)	1 (0)	3 (1)	4 (0)
Pansexual	3 (6)	14 (10)	18 (9)	46 (8)	81 (9)
Queer	7 (14)	18 (13)	32 (15)	89 (16)	146 (16)
Questioning	0 (0)	4 (3)	5 (2)	8 (1)	17 (2)
Woman-loving-woman	1 (2)	1 (1)	1 (0)	8 (1)	11 (1)
Other identity	4 (8)	2 (1)	9 (4)	15 (3)	30 (3)
Missing	4 (8)	9 (7)	12 (6)	22 (4)	47 (5)
Race/ethnicity					
White	29 (59)	79 (58)	128 (61)	318 (59)	554 (59)
Student of color	11 (22)	30 (22)	40 (19)	104 (19)	185 (20)
Missing	9 (18)	27 (20)	41 (20)	120 (22)	198 (21)

12 participants who were attending or recently had attended a two-year institution. We developed the interview protocol using the extant literature on student success and LGBTQ+ college students to explore how LGBTQ+ students felt supported within the college environment and, more specifically, who or what institutional mechanisms fostered success. The interview protocol elicited stories of

support (or a lack of support). A research team, including the first two authors, conducted the interviews. Students received a $25 gift card for participating in the interviews, which lasted from 21 to 47 minutes (average length was 31 minutes). The gender identities of the 12 participants were one cisgender man, five cisgender women, one genderqueer, one two-spirit, and four transgender students. Participants identified racially/ethnically as: one Asian or Asian American student, one Black or African American student, one multi-racial student, and nine white students. Eight two-year institutions from five states were represented among the participants.

Before analyzing the qualitative data, each interview was transcribed verbatim by a professional transcriber. Next, we uploaded all interviews into Dedoose, a web-based qualitative coding software. The first and second author read through each of the 12 transcripts line-by-line and open-coded the transcripts (Merriam, 2009). After open coding several of the transcripts, we arranged the codes to align with specific resources and used axial coding (Merriam, 2009). Following the construction of these categories, we reviewed all of the transcripts in an iterative process until no new codes were added. The first and second author coded all 12 interviews separately and reviewed each other's coding. The peer coding and debriefing process supported analytic trustworthiness (Janesick, 2011).

Limitations

While we believe the research design is robust, several limitations should be considered when interpreting the findings. First, the results may not be generalizable to all campuses given the use of convenience sampling. It is possible that students attending an LGBTQ+ and ally conference and/ or involved in LGBTQ+ networks may be more active in LGBTQ+ student communities than those not involved in these sites. Related, recruiting students through conference and networks may support our findings, especially in terms of LGBTQ+ student organizations and resources centers. These sites may have connected participants to the conference and/or LGBTQ+ networks. Second, we did not ask survey respondents for the name of their institutions and therefore cannot trace survey responses back to individual campuses; thus, multiple survey responses may represent a single campus. Third, in the survey, we relied on students' reporting knowledge of campus resources, and some students may not know if their institution possesses a particular resource, although it may be available. Finally, the qualitative sample provided rich information, however; more interview participants might provide additional insight into the lives of LGBTQ+ students attending two-year institutions.

Findings

Through review of survey and interview data about resources and sources of support, we identified four common microsystems, or campus resources, for LGBTQ+ students attending two-year institutions: LGBTQ+-specific resource centers, counseling services, career planning resources, and student organizations (e.g., Gay/Straight Alliance [GSA] and LGBTQ+-student organizations). For each resource, we show the number of students stating whether the resource exists on campus and we draw on student interview data to illuminate the importance of LGBTQ+-specific resources to two-year institution students.

Resource: LGBTQ+ Resource Center

Table 5.2 shows the number of students reporting that their institution has an LGBTQ+ resource center. Overall, 64.7% of survey respondents indicated that their campus had an LGBTQ+ resource center. Two-year institutions (18.4%) have the smallest percentage of resource centers with doctoral institutions having the highest (77.6%). Chi-square analyses results indicated that a statistically significant relationship existed between institutional type and existence of an LGBTQ+ Resource Center ($\chi^2(3) = 115.39, p < .001$).

Table 5.2 Availability of LGBTQ+ resources and services by institution type

Institution type	LGBTQ+ Resource center		LGBTQ+ Counseling services		LGBTQ+ Career planning services		Gay-straight alliance or LGBTQ+ student organization	
	No n (%)	Yes n (%)	No n (%)	Yes n (%)	No n (%)	Yes n (%)	No n (%)	Yes n (%)
Associate	40 (82)	9 (18)	35 (71)	14 (29)	47 (96)	2 (4)	7 (14)	42 (86)
Bachelor's	71 (52)	65 (48)	74 (54)	62 (46)	114 (84)	22 (16)	24 (18)	112 (82)
Master's	98 (47)	111 (53)	112 (54)	97 (46)	186 (89)	23 (11)	39 (19)	170 (81)
Doctoral	121 (22)	421 (78)	191 (35)	351 (65)	463 (85)	79 (147)	169 (31)	373 (69)
	$\chi^2(3) = 115.39^a$		$\chi^2(3) = 45.62^a$		$\chi^2(3) = 6.22$		$\chi^2(3) = 21.9^a$	

a $p < .001$.

The qualitative results suggest that LGBTQ+ resource centers play an important role in support, assistance, activism, and advocacy for queer-identified students. In our interviews, students reported that LGBTQ+ resource centers help to foster relationships with students who felt unsure about where to turn for help. As Jack, a transgender queer man, pointed out, "the director of the LGBT Center, she actually helped me get my scholarship to stay in school this semester." Another participant echoed that the director of the center on campus "was really supportive, even though it might be tough with family or other things, to keep going to school and keep progressing" (Eileen, cisgender lesbian woman). In both of these instances, this microsystem was a means for supporting the students' goal to persist at the two-year college through specific inclusive relationships with identity-specific resources.

While supporting the aims of student retention, LGBTQ+ resource centers frequently assist students with issues related to their LGBTQ identities. Meg, a cisgender lesbian woman, described her experience participating in a workshop offered through the LGBTQ+ resource center on her campus:

> I can't be as open about everything. I can't just walk up to somebody and talk to them and tell them about my life and talk to them like—after the workshop that we had the shame and vulnerability, a lot of us stayed after and talked about stuff.

Meg also reported that "there's not a lot of people that are as accepting and can talk about that kind of stuff and feel comfortable" as the professionals working in the resource center. These are just a few examples of the importance of LGBTQ+ resource centers to students with LGBTQ+-related identity-based needs and connecting students with similar experiences.

In addition to supporting individual students, LGBTQ+ resource centers engage in advocacy for campus change and support student activism. Renee, a cisgender bisexual woman, discussed how she reached out to the Director of the LGBTQ+ resource center for resources on handling a particularly challenging situation. Renee shared

> I was having issues with language and identity stuff in a couple classes, so I've been meeting with her every other week just to talk about how to get better programming and just talking through, sort of, the politics of everything, and trying to sort of raise awareness.

Like Renee, another participant shared a negative experience on campus buffered by Student Affairs professionals from the LGBTQ+ center. In this case, the campus's LGBT student organization's posters were vandalized, and in response, through the resource center LGBTQ+ students established monthly meetings with the president of the college. The resource center served as a catalyst of support for Renee and other students—an active avenue for both providing inclusion for students and feedback to the institution.

Resource: *LGBTQ+-Specific Counseling Services*

Just over a quarter of survey respondents (28.5%) from associate degree-granting institutions indicated the presence of a second microsystem—LGBTQ+ Counseling Services. Table 5.2 (LGBTQ+ Counseling Services) shows these institutions trailing bachelor's, master's, and doctoral degree-granting institutions in the availability of these services. Results of chi-square analyses indicated that a statistically significant relationship existed between institutional type and existence of an LGBTQ+ counseling services ($\chi^2(3) = 45.62, p < .001$).

Across all institutional types, two-year students reported the lowest presence of LGBTQ+-specific counseling services. Counseling centers can vary in the services that they provide to students, including specific student counseling topics and needs, so this trend could be a reflection of counseling centers choosing to include LGBTQ+-specific services without institutional direction or decision-making. The importance of having LGBTQ+-specific counseling services cannot be overstated. Some students reported suffering from depression and even contemplating suicide, and highlighted the help counseling services provided. Joey, a transgender heterosexual man, discussed the breakup of his relationship:

> She knew I was transgender and stuff, and she said she left me for transgender reasons. I had amazing support throughout the whole school. I was at a point where, unfortunately, I was thinking about suicide and stuff. I needed to reach out and get—I was so closed, and my teachers, and an amazing counselor at school. You've gotta start thinking more positive, affirming yourself.

Joey experienced a difficult breakup stemming from their transgender identity. Joey found support across the institution and specifically mentioned a counselor as being an important source of support. Narratives like Joey's illustrate how vital LGBTQ+ counseling services can support a student's well-being and persistence intentions.

Resource: LGBTQ+-Specific Career Planning Services

Table 5.2 (LGBTQ+ career planning services) shows associate degree-granting institutions (4.1%) trailing bachelor's, master's, and doctoral degree-granting institutions in the availability of LGBTQ+-specific career planning services. There was no statistically significant relationship between LGBTQ+ career counseling and institutional type ($\chi^2(3) = 6.22, p < .001$).

Several students mentioned the importance of having career counselors with awareness of LGBTQ+ issues. Barry, a cisgender gay man, approached a career advisor to see if the advisor would consider getting "OUT for Work" certified. "OUT for Work" is a national program that provides resources to career centers to support LGBTQ+ students who may face discriminatory practices during their employment search (Out for Work, n.d.). Career centers receiving an Out for Work certification receive access to online and physical resources specifically for LGBTQ+ college students and career counselors working with LGBTQ+ students. According to the most recent certification program report, 6% of certified centers identified as two-year institutions (Out for Work, n.d.). The program was no longer certified at Barry's school when he made his request, but was recertified given Barry and other students' interest in it. The same staff person became the program advisor and understood the issues facing LGBTQ+ students entering the workforce.

> It's been really, really helpful to know that I can go and—I can talk about putting Delta Lambda Phi [fraternity founded by gay men] or our gay-straight alliance on my resume and they're not gonna look at me and go, "Well, you may not wanna put those things because employers might frown upon those."

The need for these services seems clear, regardless of institutional type. The LGBTQ+ students attending two-year institutions in this study valued the interactions with general counselors and career counseling professionals. These students relied on these student services professionals to supply them with advice supporting their mental health and future employment opportunities.

Resource: *Gay/Straight Alliance or LGBTQ+ Student Organization*

The fourth microsystem we analyzed, GSA or LGBTQ+ student organization, was the most common type of resource at associates-granting institutions. Table 5.2 shows that 85.7% of study participants attending two-year institutions reported that their institution had a GSA or LGBTQ+-student organization. Results of chi-square analyses indicated that a statistically significant relationship existed between institutional type and existence of a GSA or LGBTQ+-student organization ($\chi^2(3)$ = 21.99, p < .001). Abundant evidence underlies the claim that student organizations can serve as important social support for minoritized students (see Museus & Jayakumar, 2012).

Nearly all interview participants addressed the importance of student organizations supporting LGBTQ+ students in terms of making close friends. Meg, a cisgender lesbian woman, reflected that she wanted to

> meet other people that are like me and see if I'm not the only one. . .Being in my GSA, I have at least six really close friends that I trust more than any other friend that I've made in my lifetime. They're good people. I like it. It's like, our GSA is more like a family than anything.

Jack also highlighted this type of support from his GSA and its value: "I'm more comfortable with being out because there's a club there to back me up." The GSA offered a support network for Meg, Jack, and other interviewees.

In addition to connecting students with a larger community, GSAs and LGBTQ+-specific organizations can support the institutional goal of retention. Tyler, a genderqueer asexual student illustrated this point:

> When I was thinking about quitting, I guess it was really a pretty big mixture of a few things, which weren't completely unrelated to my identity here. I really do think that if it weren't for that group, that I seriously might have ended up taking a different direction.

Here, Tyler implied that he may not have persisted during undergraduate education. Through participation in an LGBTQ+

organization, Tyler found important support during a time of need. Without this support, he may have left the institution. Postsecondary institutions can bolster student organizations with resources and leadership to provide permanence and stability to the students and overall community.

Discussion

This analysis explored the availability and importance of LGBTQ+-specific student service micro-systems across different institutional types. Our qualitative findings demonstrate the importance of four LGBTQ+-specific resources (resource centers, counseling, career planning, and student organizations) for students attending two-year institutions. Yet, our quantitative findings suggest these initiatives, except for LGBTQ+ career counseling, are significantly less common at two-year colleges than other institutional types. From an ecological perspective, the interview findings illustrate the value to students of supportive microsystems in two-year campus environments. Study results suggest that students seek out identity-specific resources for a variety of reasons including advocacy, community seeking, and source of support. Ecological theory posits that microsystems work together to create mesosystems of campus climate, which suggests the possibility of creating supportive environments for personal and academic growth. While this study did not focus on the larger exosystem and macrosystem, these contexts mattered insomuch as they may have influenced students to seek out resources important to their minoritized sexuality and gender identities. In particular, students felt that the relationships forged with various student services personnel validated them as students and LGBTQ+ people.

Compared to their peers at four-year institutions, community college students reported that in three of four cases (resource centers, LGBTQ+-specific counseling, LGBTQ+-specific career planning), they had less knowledge of supporting services existing at their school. Thus, it is possible that community college students have less access to important student services. Yet when they were available, these resources were, as noted in interviews, critical supports for students and their positive experiences, identities, and persistence. Many participants shared that LGBTQ+-specific resources have the potential to counter negative experiences, such as microaggressions and discrimination, students may experience at two-year institutions. The resources, or microsystems, identified in this study may buffer students from the negative or hostile climate on two-year campuses identified by Garvey et al. (2015). In short, the quantitative and qualitative findings indicated that for many students the institutional resources mattered.

The quantitative findings describe a landscape of two-year institutions providing fewer LGBTQ+-specific resources when compared to four-year colleges. For instance, only nine out of 49 (18.4%) two-year college students indicated their campuses offered LGBTQ+ resource centers, while almost four in five (77.7%) students at doctoral-granting institutions reported such a center being present on their campuses. The disparity in presence of LGBTQ+ resource centers may stem from the financial sensitivity two-year institutions experience annually. Pitcher, Camacho, Renn, and Woodford (2016) found that the mere presence of an LGBTQ+ center on campus signals to the student that the environment is welcoming. These signals inform LGBTQ+ students about what is available to the student. Over the last 30 years, 190 campuses (of over 5,000 postsecondary institutions in the United States) have established LGBTQ+ resource centers for students (Campus Pride Index, 2017). Of the 190 campuses, few two-year institutions are represented. The intention of these resource centers is to provide support for LGBTQ+ students; without a center, students must find co-curricular activities, education, and connections with the LGBTQ+ community on their own.

Students attending two-year institutions often expect to transfer to a four-year institution or graduate and enter the workforce (Jenkins & Fink, 2016). These expectations call for an expansion of resources, such as LGBTQ+ counseling and career counseling centers within two-year institutions—resources that can assist in helping students think about academic paths through four-year institutions to careers or developing other employment strategies. These types of resources are essential for student success. While career counseling resources specifically for LGBTQ+ students were the least likely to be reported as a service (with 13.4% of students across institutional types indicating such a resource exists on their campus), only 4.1% of students at two-year institutions were aware of LGBTQ+ specific support for their professional ambitions, leaving these students without clearly communicated institutional support.

As our data indicate, student-led organizations such as GSAs are most common at two-year institutions (85.8% of two-year institution students reporting awareness of such a group), illustrating that students at two-year institutions may be more likely to encounter support from their peers than from a formal institutional resource. There is nothing inherently wrong with peer support, but the institutional decision (or default) to leave support for LGBTQ+ students to their peers could shape students' perceptions of the campus climate. While an important resource, relying on peer-interaction as the most likely support roots an individual's relationship with LGBTQ+ support at the microsystem level, instead of being formalized through the institutional meso- and exosystems.

Implications for Practice and Future Research

Resources and personnel to staff LGBTQ+ resources for college students are critical to LGBTQ+ student persistence for a number of reasons. First, consistently across LGBTQ+ climate studies (conducted primarily within four-year institutions) findings suggest campus environments are inherently heteronormative. Heteronormativity privileges conformity to heterosexual roles, pervades the dominant culture, and operationalizes through students' behavior at their individual institutions (Kitzinger, 2005; Misawa, 2010). Resource centers, student organizations for students minoritized by gender and sexual identities, and LGBTQ+-supportive counselors and career counselors create counter-spaces, microsystems that resist and buffer against pervasive forces of heteronormativity. Given the relative ubiquity of student organizations compared to resource centers and LGBTQ+-supportive counseling at two-year institutions, we recommend that these colleges bolster student organizations with resources and leadership, which, in turn, provide stability to counter-spaces in the ecosystem.

Resource constraints and organizational structures yield specific challenges in creating and sustaining student support resources, including those for LGBTQ+ students and communities. Two-year institutions are often seen as vehicles for fulfilling the college completion agenda and face scrutiny in how public appropriations are used (Crookston & Hooks, 2012). Unlike four-year institutions, two-year institutions generally do not have access to alternative forms of funding, such as overhead from federal research grants and tuition differentials charged to out-of-state students. Lacking these additional funding options, two-year institutions must be strategic and creative in how they distribute funds to nonacademic units like student services (Tollefson, 2009), doing the same or more with less financial flexibility than other institutional types (Hirt, 2006). While our first recommendation is that two-year institutions should consider allocating resources for LGBTQ+ resource centers to serve as hubs for support and services, we recognize that it is unlikely that many resource-constrained campuses can take up this charge. There are, however, distinctive characteristics of the community college that can be leveraged to increase support and improve the ecosystem for LGBTQ+ students.

Two-year colleges demonstrate a higher degree of collaboration and integration between academic and Student Affairs, exhibiting a commitment to but more limited focus on the student experience beyond the classroom than more traditional four-year schools (Knight, 2014). Professionals providing extra- and co-curricular support for students typically play multiple roles throughout the institution (Hirt, 2006; Ozaki & Hornak, 2014), a circumstance that poses both challenges and opportunities for providing identity-specific student supports. Many four-year institutions operate their LGBTQ+ resource centers with the help of an invested faculty or staff member, who provides stability and organization history as a support structure for student-led communities. The close relationships across academic and Student Affairs units in the two-year institution might facilitate this structure, as might the cross-functional ("many hats") roles of student support staff. Hiring undergraduate staff, instead of relying only on volunteers, to organize LGBTQ+ activities is less costly than hiring professional staff and providing meaningful student employment.

Other possible alternatives would be to identify physical or digital space for LGBTQ+ groups to gather and connect as a substantiation of the community needs and legitimacy as part of the campus culture, and identify and train willing and appropriate faculty and staff interested in supporting LGBTQ+ individuals and communities. Finally, the community-based nature of two-year institutions might make it possible to create partnerships with LGBTQ+ resource centers housed within local school districts, nonprofit organizations, or neighboring four-year colleges. Partnering with local entities can introduce students to community resources of which they may be unaware and be useful in developing support networks. Furthermore, these partnerships may benefit student services at two-year institutions by creating additional resources that they can direct their students to during times of experiencing distress and needing support.

Implications for Future Research

In addition to addressing methodological limitations addressed earlier, several ideas for future research emerge from this analysis.

First, individual campus climate studies at two-year institutions are essential to understanding the extant culture and to understanding whether community colleges, as open access institutions, do in fact support all students and their development. More studies about the LGBTQ+ student experience at two-year institutions will yield valuable and rich information about persistence, retention, and marginalization. Further, evaluating how students use LGBTQ+ specific resources will provide Student Affairs professionals and institutional leadership with an understanding of how students access these resources and how they contribute to the student's ability to navigate the two-year campus and beyond. We believe that it is especially important to consider how students' identities beyond gender and sexuality may shape their use of resources as well as decisions not to use resources. Finally, we recommend undertaking a longitudinal study of LGBTQ+ students entering two-year institutions through graduation, transfer to four-year institution, and beyond to understand the potential long-term impact of LGBTQ+ resource availability on graduation and retention metrics.

Conclusion

This study documents from the perspective of LGBTQ+ students the presence of LGBTQ+ resources and their importance to students' identities, challenges, and success. The findings establish the value LGBTQ+ specific resources hold at two-year institutions. Our quantitative results illuminate a discrepancy in the availability of these types of resources among different higher educational institutional types. LGBTQ+ students, like other minoritized students, benefit from resources to support their postsecondary academic and social success.

References

American Association of Community Colleges (2017). *Fast facts from our fact sheet.* Retrieved from http://www.aacc. nche.edu/AboutCC/Pages/fastfactsfactsheet.aspx

Bailey, T., & Morest, V. S. (2006). *Defending the community college equity agenda.* Baltimore, MD: Johns Hopkins University Press.

Bailey, T. R., & Alfonso, M. (2005). *Paths to persistence: An analysis of research on program effectiveness at community colleges.* New Agenda Series. Indianapolis, IN: Lumina Foundation.

Beemyn, G. (2012). The experiences and needs of transgender community college students. *Community College Journal of Research and Practice, 36*(7), 504–510.

Bieschke, K. J., Eberz, A. B., & Wilson, D. (2000). Empirical investigations of the gay, lesbian, and bisexual college student. In V. A. Wall & N. J. Evans (Eds.), *Toward acceptance: Sexual orientation issues on campus* (pp. 29–58). Washington, DC: American College Personnel Association.

Bound, J., Lovenheim, M., & Turner, S. E. (2009). *Why have college completion rates declined?* NBER (National Bureau of Economic Research) working paper 15566.

Bronfenbrenner, U. (1979). *The ecology of human development: Experiments by design and nature.* Cambridge, MA: Harvard University Press.

Bronfenbrenner, U. (1993). The ecology of cognitive development: Research models and fugitive findings. In R. H. Wozniak & K. W. Fischer (Eds.), *Development in context: Acting and thinking in specific environments* (pp. 3–44). Hillsdale, NJ: Erlbaum.

Bronfenbrenner, U. (1995). Developmental ecology through space and time: A future perspective. In P. Moen & G. H. Elder Jr (Eds.), *Examining lives in context: Perspectives on the ecology of human development* (pp. 619–647). Washington, DC: American Psychological Association.

Brown, R. D., Clarke, B., Gortmaker, V., & Robinson-Keilig, R. (2004). Assessing the campus climate for gay, lesbian, bisexual, and transgender (GLBT) students using a multiple perspectives approach. *Journal of College Student Development, 45*(1), 8–26.

Calcagno, J. C., Bailey, T., Jenkins, D., Kienzl, G., & Leinbach, T. (2008). Community college student success: What institutional characteristics make a difference? *Economics of Education Review, 27*(6), 632–645.

Campus Pride Index (2017). *Community colleges.* Retrieved from http://www.campusprideindex.org/about/default.aspx

Crisp, G., & Taggart, A. (2013). Community college student success programs: A synthesis, critique, and research agenda. *Community College Journal of Research and Practice, 36*(2), 114–130.

Crookston, A., & Hooks, G. (2012). Community colleges, budget cuts, and jobs: The impact of community colleges on employment growth in rural US counties, 1976–2004. *Sociology of Education, 85*(4), 350–372.

Dowd, A. C., & Cheslock, J. (2006). Equity and efficiency of community college appropriations: The role of local financing. *Review of Higher Education, 29,* 167–194.

Garvey, J. C., Taylor, J. L., & Rankin, S. (2015). An examination of campus climate for LGBTQ community college students. *Community College Journal of Research and Practice, 39*(6), 527–541. doi:10.1080/10668926.2013.861374

Goldrick-Rab, S. (2010). Challenges and opportunities for improving community college student success. *Review of Educational Research, 80*(3), 437–469.

Greene, T., Marti, C., & McClenney, K. (2008). The effort-outcome gap: differences for African American and Hispanic community college students in student engagement and academic achievement. *The Journal of Higher Education, 79*(5), 513–539.

Hirt, J. B. (2006). *Where you work matters*. Lanham, MA: University Press of America.

Ivory, B. T. (2005). LGBT students in community college: Characteristics, challenges, and recommendations. In R. L. Sanlo (Ed.), *Gender identity and sexual orientation: Research, policy, and personal perspectives. New directions for student services* (Vol. 111, pp. 25–40). San Francisco, CA: Jossey-Bass.

Janesick, V. J. (2011). *Stretching exercises for qualitative researchers* (3rd ed.). Thousand Oaks, CA: Sage.

Jenkins, D., & Fink, J. (2016). *Tracking transfer: New measures of institutional and state effectiveness in helping community college students attain bachelor's degrees*. New York, NY: Community College Research Center.

Johnson, R. B., Onwuegbuzie, A. J., & Turner, L. A. (2007). Toward a definition of mixed methods research. *Journal of Mixed Methods Research, 1*(2), 112–133.

Karp, M. M. (2011). *Toward a new understanding of non-academic student support: Four mechanisms encouraging positive student outcomes in the community college*. New York, NY: Community College Research Center.

Katsinas, S., & Tollefson, T. (2009). *Funding and access issues in public higher education: A community college perspective*. Education Policy Center. Tuscaloosa, AL: University of Alabama.

Kitzinger, C. (2005). Heteronormativity in action: Reproducing the heterosexual nuclear family in after-hours medical calls. *Social Problems, 52*(4), 477–498.

Knight, A. (2014). Excellence in community college student affairs. In C. C. Ozaki, A. M. Hornak, & C. J. Lunceford (Eds.), *Supporting student affairs professionals. New directions for community colleges* (Vol. 166, pp. 5–12). San Francisco, CA: Jossey-Bass.

Leck, G. M. (1998). An oasis: The LGBT student group on a commuter campus. In R. L. Sanlo (Ed.), *Working with lesbian, gay, bisexual, and transgender college students: A handbook for faculty and administrators* (pp. 373–388). Westport, CT: Greenwood.

Leider, S. (2000). *Sexual minorities on community college campuses*. Los Angeles, CA: ERIC Clearinghouse for Community Colleges. Retrieved from ERIC Document Reproduction Service.

Leider, S. (2012). LGBTQ people on community college campuses: A 20-year review. *Community College Journal of Research and Practice, 36*(7), 471–447.

Manning, P., Pring, L., & Glider, P. (2012). Relevance of campus climate for alcohol and other drug use among LGBTQ community college students: A statewide qualitative assessment. *Community College Journal of Research and Practice, 36*, 494–503.

Mayhew, M. J., Rockenbach, A. N., Bowman, N. A., Seifert, T. A., Wolniak, G. C., Pascarella, E. T., & Terenzini, P. Y. (2016). *How college affects students (Vol. 3): 21st century evidence that higher education works*. San Francisco, CA: Jossey-Bass.

Meier, K. (2013). Community college mission in historical perspective. In J. S. Levin & S. T. Kater (Eds.), *Understanding community colleges* (pp. 3–18). New York, NY: Routledge.

Merriam, S. B. (2009). *Qualitative research: A guide to design and implementation.* San Francisco, CA: Jossey-Bass.

Misawa, M. (2010). Racist and homophobic bullying in adulthood: Narratives from gay men of color in higher education. *New Horizons in Adult Education and Human Resource Development, 24*(1), 7–23.

Museus, S. D., & Jayakumar, U. M. (Eds.). (2012). *Creating campus cultures: Fostering success among racially diverse student populations.* New York, NY: Routledge.

Nitecki, E. M. (2011). The power of the program: How the academic program can improve community college student success. *Community College Review, 39*(2), 98–120.

Out for Work. (n.d.). *Welcome to the career center certification.* Retrieved from http://outforwork.org/resources/career_center/

Ozaki, C. C., & Hornak, A. M. (2014). Excellence within student affairs: Understanding the practice of integrating academic and student affairs. In C. C. Ozaki, A. M. Hornak, & C. J. Lunceford (Eds.), *Supporting student affairs professionals. New directions for community colleges* (Vol. 166, pp. 79–84). San Francisco, CA: Jossey-Bass.

Pascarella, E. T., & Terenzini, P. T. (2005). *How college affects students* (2nd ed.). San Francisco, CA: Jossey-Bass.

Pitcher, E. N., Camacho, T. P., Renn, K. A., & Woodford, M. R. (2016). Affirming policies, programs, and supportive services: Using an organizational perspective to understand LGBTQ+ college student success. *Journal of Diversity in Higher Education,* 11(2), 117–132. doi:10.1037/dhe0000048

Rankin, S., Blumenfeld, W. J., Weber, G. N., & Frazer, S. J. (2010). *State of higher education for LGBT people: Campus Pride 2010 national college climate survey.* Charlotte, NC: Campus Pride.

Renn, K. A., & Arnold, K. D. (2003). Reconceptualizing research on college student peer culture. *Journal of Higher Education, 74*(3), 261–291.

Sanlo, R. (2012). Guest editor's introduction. *Community College Journal of Research and Practice, 36*(7), 467–470.

Sanlo, R., & Espinoza, L. (2012). Risk and retention: Are LGBTQ students staying in your community college? *Community College Journal of Research and Practice, 36*(7), 475–481.

Strange, C. C., & Banning, J. H. (2015). *Designing for learning: Creating campus environments for student success.* San Francisco, CA: John Wiley & Sons.

Taylor, J. L., Dockendorff, K. J., & Inselman, K. (2018). Decoding the digital campus climate for prospective LGBTQ+ community colleges students. *Community College Journal of Research and Practice, 42*(3), 155–170.

Tollefson, T. A. (2009). Community college governance, funding, and accountability: A century of issues and trends. *Community College Journal of Research and Practice, 33*(3–4), 386–402.

Wood, J. L., & Harris, F., III. (2013). The community college survey of men: An initial validation of the instrument's non-cognitive outcomes construct. *Community College Journal of Research and Practice, 37*(4), 333–338.

Woodford, M. R., & Kulick, A. (2015). Academic and social integration on campus among sexual minority students: The impacts of psychological and experiential campus climate. *American Journal of Community Psychology, 55*, 13–24.

Zamani-Gallaher, E. M., & Choudhuri, D. D. (2011). A primer on LGBTQ students at community colleges: Considerations for research and practice. In E. M. Cox & J. S. Watson (Eds.), *Marginalized students. New directions for community colleges* (Vol. 155, pp. 35–49). San Francisco, CA: Jossey-Bass.

Zamani-Gallaher, E. M., & Choudhuri, D. D. (2016). Tracing LGBTQ community college students' experiences. In C. C. Ozaki, & R. L. Spaid (Eds.), *Marginalized students. New directions for community colleges* (Vol. 174, pp. 47–63). San Francisco, CA: Jossey-Bass.

6 The Completion Agenda Impact on Student Affairs Practice in Community Colleges

Patrick W. Gill and Laura M. Harrison

The Completion Agenda Impact on Student Affairs Practice in Community Colleges

The Completion Agenda is the educational and political movement that arose in 2010 and concentrated on increasing the number of college graduates with workforce credentials. Similar student success efforts had existed prior to the Completion Agenda (O'Banion, 2010). In fact, we argue that such student success initiatives took on added importance following the Great Recession, prior to a time when the Completion Agenda was a widespread phenomenon. As a movement, however, the Completion Agenda introduced significant changes that transformed the higher education landscape. Amidst this transformation, community colleges have arguably experienced the greatest change.

While all institution types have been asked to support the Completion Agenda, community colleges have shouldered more of the responsibility. Experts believed that increasing completion rates would need to begin with retooling unemployed workers (Mullin, 2010) and providing support for historically underrepresented populations (Bragg & Durham, 2012; Dassance, 2011), largely community college endeavors. To meet national goals and workforce needs, community colleges, states, and nonprofits have also pushed for expedited time to completion (Couturier, 2012; Lumina Foundation, 2013). Scholarship related to the community college role has likewise considered ways to achieve these ends (Bailey, Jaggars, & Jenkins, 2015; Jenkins & Cho, 2013; Pennington & Milliron, 2010). Amidst sweeping changes, Student Affairs on community college campuses have received little attention. We believe that the work of Student Affairs is integral to the overarching goal of student success; fully realized Student Affairs contribute to the growth and development of individuals with lifelong value.

This study considers the function of Student Affairs within the Completion Agenda by analyzing Student Affairs educators' beliefs about their work related to the value others attribute to it. The term Student Affairs educator is used to describe personnel whose work is dedicated to helping students develop and providing them with meaningful learning opportunities (ACPA & NASPA, 2010; Helfgot, 2005; Munsch & Cortez, 2014; Tyrell, 2014). Student Affairs educators consistently uphold the meaning of their work and how it directly contributes to student development (Hirt, 2006); however, community college Student Affairs are rarely prioritized at the institutional, state, or national levels. This neglect is heightened by the neoliberal impulse to focus on speed as opposed to the quality of the student experience. Fundamental differences in how Student Affairs educators and community college administrators value noncognitive learning challenge the vitality of student development. We argue that if student development continues to be an afterthought, we risk diminishing key aspects of student learning that take place outside of the classroom.

We begin with a literature review of the topics central to our study, in particular, the Completion Agenda and Student Affairs. Next, we frame our discussion within the theoretical lens of neoliberalism. Following, we present our student and themes that arose from our findings. We conclude with limitations, a discussion, and future research.

The Completion Context

The Completion Agenda built upon the community college access mission and called for increasing rates of college graduates (O'Banion, 2010). Although organizations, like the College Board (Hughes, 2013) and the Lumina Foundation (Lumina Foundation, 2013), had shifted their focus to college completion in the mid-2000s, the Completion Agenda became a centralized issue in the aftermath of the Great Recession, in large part due to calls for action from the White House (Bernanke, 2008; Malcolm, 2009; Office of the Press Secretary, 2009). *Democracy's colleges: Call to action* (AACC, 2010), signed by leaders of organizations representing America's community colleges, presented a united vision that would guide the completion movement. In *Democracy's colleges*, national leaders declared, "We. . .recognize and celebrate the colleges' central role in ensuring an educated U.S. citizenry and a globally competitive workforce" (para. 1). Completion efforts were expected to align with the purposes articulated within the document moving forward.

Community College Student Affairs, Student Development, and Student Success

Student affairs, with roots tracing back to *The Student Personnel Point of View* of 1937 and 1949 (ACPA, 2014a, 2014b), refer to the discipline practiced by those in higher education who work with students and on their behalf (Helfgot, 2005). Student Affairs have sought to address the needs of students at critical junctures in their cognitive, psychosocial, moral, physical, and spiritual growth. The field has advanced as a result of student development theory (Creamer, 1989; Helfgot, 2005; Strange, 1994; Wimbish, Bumphus, & Helfgot, 1995). While the field of Student Affairs has developed considerably since the early- to mid-20th century, community college Student Affairs have lacked the direction and purpose seen at four-year institutions. In using the term "Student Affairs," we are aware that Student Affairs have historical weight but is also not standard across institutions, especially community colleges ("student services" being prominent).

Community college Student Affairs have had to overcome challenges (Elsner & Ames, 1983; Medsker, 1960), have debated different models of delivery (Dassance, 1984; Keyser, 1989; O'Banion, Thurston, & Gulden, 1972), and have been slow to organize professionally (Floyd, 1991; Garrett, Bragg, & Makela, 2006; Keyser, 1985). In large part, it still appears disorganized due to disharmony with four-year institutions. Student development theory has excluded community colleges or been applied as an afterthought (Helfgot, 2005). Research has traditionally been informed by the experiences of traditional, White, male, upper-class, residential students (Wimbish et al., 1995). In addition, student success theories, like Tinto (1975, 1986, 1993) and Astin (1984, 1993, 1999), have limited application or do not consider the unique experiences of community college student populations (Ozaki, 2016). To serve as an example, student involvement (Astin, 1984) is foundational at residential four-year institutions; however, community college scholars and practitioners have intentionally set their work apart because students cannot devote the same time and energy to their academic pursuits (Helfgot, 1998).

The Center for Community College Student Engagement (2004) recognized that community college students are different from four-year students, that they have demands outside of class that prevent them from spending an ample amount of time on campus for engagement to happen spontaneously. As a result, the center's work and corresponding survey (CCSSE) has direct application and regularly surfaces in student success discussions. Still, scholars have yet to embrace a unifying framework that can be applied following the onset of the Completion Agenda.

Wang (2017) addressed this very issue in a recently proposed theoretical model on student success, which is grounded in the metaphorical concept of *momentum*. She stated:

> I anchor the momentum concept in community college students' academic and enrollment behaviors, experiences within the classroom, and motivational attitudes and beliefs. These facets intersect and intertwine as students navigate the curriculum, which reflects the unique nature of how community college students engage with their postsecondary educational experience, as compared with their four-year college counterparts whose engagement with college tends to span more evenly across the curricular and co-curricular domains.
>
> (p. 260)

Wang categorized the approaches that surface in literature as intensity-based, milestone-based, and pattern-based. The community college's overarching completion function, student demographics, and student goals informed this holistic model. Paralleling this work is the Bill and Melinda Gates Foundation's Completion by Design initiative (Pennington & Milliron, 2010) and policy changes that have been proposed to increase completion (Couturier, 2012; National Conference for State Legislators, 2017).

Within the student success discussion are ongoing debates on *how* this takes place. Wang (2017) acknowledged the centrality of the classroom in the student success model of momentum and provided rationale for this line of thinking. She even acknowledged that areas outside of the classroom could merit exploration: "These out-of-classroom domains may be missed opportunities where community colleges could expand efforts to increase momentum and learning" (p. 291). However, we believe that how students build momentum is not the critical question. Completion by Design, through its *Loss/Momentum Framework*, sought to assist community colleges in redesigning all aspects of the college-going experience to reduce barriers and facilitate momentum. Within this framework and through similar work on guided pathways (Jenkins & Cho, 2013; O'Banion, 2011), "how" becomes the focus, whereas "why" is taken at face value or not considered at all.

Due to how much has been written and shared about community college completion, we have reached a point where we risk accepting completion as a value in itself. Harbour and Smith (2016) challenged the completion narrative from the perspective that the vision is largely economic and rooted in a functionalist history, one that sees community colleges serving the "central needs of society" (p. 103). In response, they consider community colleges from the standpoint of democracy as problem-solving. Their overarching critique aligns with our view that the Completion Agenda is shortsighted due to its myopic focus on the economy. Fundamental beliefs guiding our study ask that we question the extent to which student development has become secondary to student completion efficiency, commentary that seeks to inform the larger discussion of the community college purpose today.

Neoliberalism

Neoliberalism provides important context for understanding the Completion Agenda generally as well as this study specifically. Neoliberalism is a hotly contested term (Thorsen, 2010); however, it is understood to include "a valorization of private enterprise. . .and the deployment of 'enterprise models' that would allow the state itself to 'run like a business'" (Ferguson, 2010, p. 170). As one might expect, public institutions provide the foil for this private enterprise valorization. Pure advocates of neoliberalism seek to diminish public goods and services, ultimately eliminating them in favor of privatized replacements. Efforts to repeal the Affordable Care Act and support for school vouchers provide good examples of this line of thinking.

The milder version of neoliberalism involves less of a repeal and replace impulse and more of the run public services like a business idea. Sometimes begrudgingly, neoliberal enthusiasts acknowledge the need for some public institutions but extol the market values of self-interest and competition as the correct drivers. Opponents of neoliberalism often acknowledge market values as appropriate for business but argue public goods, like education, are existentially different from the sale of consumer products. Vollmer's (2010) *Schools Cannot Do It Alone* provided a particularly illustrative example of this line of thinking. Vollmer told the story of being a typical outsider speaking to a group of teachers about how they could use his business savvy to run their school more effectively. He explained that a teacher asked him if he only used the finest quality ingredients in his ice-cream business. He eagerly agreed that he did, particularly, in his very popular blueberry ice cream. The teacher asked him to consider that public schools do not get to select which proverbial blueberries they serve, making the comparison between a private corporation and a public service limited at best. The teacher spoke of the pride she took in serving all the "blueberries," including the ones bruised by life and therefore struggling at times.

The community college could just as easily have been the backdrop for Vollmer's (2010) story. Hailed as access institutions that accept nearly everyone, community colleges enroll many students who attended underresourced K-12 schools. As a result, many of these students are not college-ready, a term Conley (2008) defined as the ability to complete college-level work without remediation. Given the persistent segregation in the K-12 school system, students who are not college-ready are disproportionately low-income due to what Welton and Williams (2015) referred to as a lack of college-going culture in high-poverty high schools. As Welton and Williams explained, poor students often attend schools that have been labeled failure factories and thus spend much of their time in rote learning activities designed to improve test scores. In contrast, wealthy students enjoy schools with rigorous curricula, guidance counselors with reasonable caseloads, and easily accessible information about college. This segregation continues at the postsecondary education level with wealthy students overrepresented at the most prestigious universities (Hearn & Rosinger, 2014) and low-income students overrepresented in community colleges (Mellow & Heelan, 2014). While race and class do not correlate perfectly, years of systemic racism have resulted in the economic disenfranchisement of African American and Latinx populations.

At this juncture, it is important to understand where neoliberalism intersects with both racism and classism. As Hamer and Lang (2015) explained, neoliberalism gained prominence in the 1970s as politicians sold a rollback of the gains afforded by the Civil Rights and labor movements in the package of free markets. Higher education was no exception as public subsidies were slashed and tuition rose. Further, politicians extolled the benefits of marketable skills over classic liberal arts education, a practice that has only grown in recent years. As a contemporary example of this phenomenon, Florida Governor Rick Scott proposed providing tuition discounts for majors in high demand fields (STEM, among others), as opposed to the humanities and others that are not (Hamer & Lang, 2015; Weissmann, 2012).

Although never stated overtly, the logical consequence of the neoliberal impulse in a segregated education system is that students at elite institutions (disproportionately White, Asian, and/or wealthy) receive the benefits of a liberal education with an emphasis on student development, while students at community colleges (disproportionately African American, Latinx, and/or poor) are tracked toward vocational programs. To be sure, there is nothing wrong with vocational education; all people need practical skills that can land them gainful employment. The wrongness stems from the de facto segregation that allows some students college experiences that develop them as whole people while others are trained to be means to corporate leaders' ends. Harbour and Smith (2016) raised this concern specifically in terms of the Completion Agenda as a policy that positions community college students as valuable solely for their role in workforce development. They argued compellingly for a definition of democracy that includes civic engagement in problem-solving in addition to gainful employment.

Accordingly, the theoretical underpinnings of the current study challenge a narrative that values college completion for economic means alone. Students often come to experience civic engagement, along with numerous other inter- and intrapersonal benefits, from Student Affairs education. Now that the Completion Agenda has come to fruition, we wonder how Student Affairs educators at community colleges have balanced its requirements with students' non-economic needs. In the section that follows, we explain the study's development and implementation in the context of neoliberalism as a theoretical framework.

Research Design

Community college Student Affairs educators have not been given adequate voice in the Completion Agenda. As Student Affairs educators work directly with students in terms of their development, they have certain expertise that cannot be gained by those removed from day-to-day functions. Admittedly, community college administrators possess qualities that are markedly different from those at different institution types (Hirt, 2006). Even though community college Student Affairs educators feel marginalized when compared to their four-year counterparts, they similarly embrace their work and find it meaningful. As a result, much can be gained by learning about the Completion Agenda and its impact on student development through community college Student Affairs professionals.

The following research questions guided this study: (1) What changes in co-curricular education did community college Student

Affairs educators experience at the onset of the Completion Agenda? (2) How do community college Student Affairs educators view the purpose of their profession within the Completion Agenda? (3) Within the Completion Agenda, how do community college Student Affairs educators feel their work is valued at institutions where they work or have worked? (4) And what tensions exist for community college Student Affairs educators related to educational or professional values and institutional expectations?

Methodology

Qualitative research was used because it considers how participants make meaning and it addresses multiple, complex variables (Creswell, 2013). Since the goal of this research was to understand the perspectives and worldviews of those involved, a basic interpretive methodology was applied (Merriam, 2002). As with all qualitative research, the researcher acted as key instrument. The researcher (Gill) conducted interviews and gathered documents, and, following, data were inductively analyzed to determine themes. To ensure the findings were congruent with reality, measures that were used to establish validity (Merriam, 1995) included member checking, triangulation, reflexivity, and peer debriefing.

Sample

Criterion sampling was used in order to identify participants for this study (Creswell, 2013; Patton, 2002). Criteria included community college affiliation, Student Affairs or college student personnel background, mid- to senior-level administrative responsibilities, and work duties concerned with student development at the outset of the Completion Agenda. The sample was limited to community college institutions in Ohio. Ohio warrants study because it is a performance-based funding state, it has a strong community college organization (Ohio Association of Community Colleges), and it has supported noteworthy completion initiatives.

Data Collection

After IRB approval, data were primarily gathered through in-depth (60-minute), semi-structured interviews with 12 participants at 10 different institutions (see Participant Table in Appendix A). Interviews were conducted at each participant's place of work (see Interview

Protocol in Appendix B). Brinkmann and Kvale (2015) described the qualitative research interview as one that "attempts to understand the world from the subjects' point of view, to unfold the meaning of their experiences, [and] to uncover their lived world prior to scientific explanations" (p. 3). Data were also gathered through documents. Documents can be used to provide background information on the site, program, or population (Marshall & Rossman, 2011). In this study, each participants' respective Campus Completion Plan provided insight into student development and co-curricular education within the college's overarching completion goals.

Data Analysis

Data analysis incorporated steps from Creswell (2014) and Merriam and Tisdell (2016). We used ATLAS.ti to organize, code, and categorize data from transcripts and documents. Each piece of raw data was analyzed through close reading and annotation. Data were then coded through open coding. Codes were grouped into a master list through axial coding, wherein categories/subcategories and corresponding data were organized beneath each applicable research question. From this information, findings made and applied cross-case analysis to determine larger themes that had emerged across the research questions.

Findings

Participants shared their experience regarding the Completion Agenda's impact on their work. All participants' names have been replaced with pseudonyms, and every institution has been replaced with a pseudoplace to honor confidentiality. Of the 12 participants, six were female and six were male, 11 identified as White and one African American, and their professional experiences ranged from eight years to 36 years. Also, individuals fell into three broad categories: *Student Affairs administrators* (senior Student Affairs officers or directly reporting to that role), *student life administrators* (student life or student involvement staff), and *student success administrators* (student success and completion staff).

Themes

Salient themes arose, which included: (1) being on message about the Completion Agenda; (2) acute attention to the work of academic affairs and Student Affairs; (3) importance of college culture; (4) focus at the beginning and end of the student experience; and (5) occupying a minor place in the Campus Completion Plan.

Being on Message about the Completion Agenda

Participants expressed support for national completion efforts and had prioritized administrative responsibilities at their own institutions accordingly. The majority of participants believed that the goals established by the Completion Agenda were something that Student Affairs' offices should embrace. Dave stated, "It's something we should probably have been doing all along." Others echoed this sentiment, arguing that their offices should be concerned with retention. Alicia said:

> I actually appreciate the Completion Agenda...I think, in higher education, for a long time we were throwing a lot of things at the wall and hoping that they work. I think it is forcing us into more of an area of focus on completion, which really should be our job.

Participants described how the Completion Agenda marked a shift from the access funnel, which did not fully respond to student needs. In this manner, the Completion Agenda provided an opportunity to engage in work that is foundational to Student Affairs but had not always been a priority.

Participants expressed few concerns with the institutions where they work. They largely described initiatives in matter-of-fact terms and presented few challenges to college goals. Student Affairs and student success administrators demonstrated a keen awareness to the connection between completion and sustainability. Alicia said:

> One of the things that we've done well, actually, is kind of zeroed in on those things that will maximize the amount of resources flowing into the institution, and then allow us to do the other co-curricular things that we know support student success.

Seven participants described changes resulting from performance-based funding, and all participants discussed funding in some manner. In addition, most of the participants were attuned to expectations from the state and other external organizations, demonstrating an appreciation for institutional demands within the greater higher education context.

*Acute Attention to the Work of Academic Affairs
and Student Affairs*

Several participants framed their work in relation to academic affairs. They spoke about their role as supporting academic affairs, the push to connect co-curricular education to the classroom, and the need to validate what takes place outside of the classroom.

One insight that arose from this study was how Student Affairs educators perceived their role as supporting academics. Debbie described nonfaculty as the "guide on the side." Coline explained that Student Affairs act as the "supporting cast." Alicia said, "Really, when you think of it. . .that defines the type of work that you do because we are here to basically ensure that faculty can teach, and then we handle everything else." This belief clashes with *The Student Learning Imperative*, which states the work of Student Affairs is equally important to academic affairs due to an emphasis on learning, not location (ACPA, 1996). While this observation could be a community college phenomenon due to differences between largely residential (four-year) and commuter (community college) cultures, the extent to which participants aligned with this belief was noteworthy.

Participants in this study argued that co-curricular education needs to be unavoidable, something recent scholarship has also encouraged (Center for Community College Student Engagement, 2009; McClenney, 2013; O'Banion, 2011). Seven participants described how their institutions have intentionally connected co-curricular education back to the classroom. The primary way this happens is by making outside-of-class opportunities relevant to the curriculum. According to participants, community college educators need to consider students' competing demands. Since community college students are typically not residential, it is not realistic or arguably in their best interest to expect them to attend outside-of-class activities. Coline said:

> With commuter students it's very hard to keep their attention outside of class or hold them on campus beyond class for a social activity. We've tried to combine the social and the academic and partner with faculty to put on some programming they would find attractive.

Even though participants acknowledged the value of student involvement within their student development philosophies, they recognized limitations in making opportunities available due to the populations they serve.

Participants also expressed a need to be good stewards of financial resources. They warned that times have changed and spending with little educational benefit is no longer acceptable. Lynn stated, "I'm sounding like an old prude, but I sometimes think we shoot ourselves in the foot by having events that would seem to be childish or useless." Student life administrators, like Dario and Henry, described how they now need to take an extra step to justify spending, especially for large-scale events. At a time when budgets are tight, Student Affairs administrators have learned to justify spending using return on investment measures.

Importance of College Culture

The need for Student Affairs educators to justify their own existence surfaced throughout the study. Over 20 years ago, the Traverse City Statement urged Student Affairs professionals to "demonstrate their contributions to the achievement of student and institutional goals" (Keyser, 1985, p. 35). Statements like these are common and have not changed considerably over time. Along those same lines, Joseph said, "Maybe we're not center stage, but we are definitely the strong guy on the side to compliment the academic setting. I think we do have to fight to remind people of the importance of why we're here." Similarly, Dave said, "I think this is a time for Student Affairs to stand up. . . It's a time to fully flex the muscle in terms of, 'This is what we do.'"

Whether or not participants felt a need to validate their work was directly related to institutional culture. Dave, for instance, held the belief that his area is able to have a meaningful impact because the President and other senior administrators have a student-centered philosophy. Others, like Lynn and Coline, could only get faculty to see their value in the midst of a crisis or by reinforcing their worth through messaging. The value of Student Affairs extends to whether or not students have a voice at the institution. At Trumbull, a section of the board meeting is devoted to students; as a result, student development takes on added importance across the institution. In order to reflect Student Affairs in the best light, participants expressed a need to share relevant data. Alicia acknowledged that building a culture of evidence is not a new idea; however, challenges exist in translating their work into metrics that others will find meaningful, like retention and completion. Concerns that participants noted suggest that Student Affairs' perception is an ongoing challenge.

Focus at the Beginning and End of the Student Experience

With the shift toward retention and completion, a more intentional focus has been placed at the beginning and end of the student experience. Community college research, in particular, the Survey of Entering Student Engagement (Center for Community College Student Engagement, 2008), demonstrated how early connections made by faculty, staff, and administrators have a significant impact on persistence. Dave, Debbie, Aaron, Coline, and Dario oversee or play a major role in new student orientation at their respective institutions. As a result, they devote a considerable amount of attention to the onboarding process.

Within the efficiency model, there has surprisingly been more emphasis on slowing down a student's connection to the institution to ensure that the student encounters the right learning opportunities from the outset. Erin described the process in pregnancy terms: The first trimester is the application, the second trimester is orientation, and the third trimester is the first semester. Lynn and Dave explained that they are each working not only to streamline the process to make fewer touchpoints, but also to make those connections more meaningful. Dave said, "We talk about [onboarding] from the success marker standpoint. It actually takes us a little longer to do it this way, but it's a return on an investment." Even though onboarding processes are customized to every institution, most of the participants were concerned with front-loading information in hopes that it will have some lasting impact.

Along with the front-end of the student experience, Student Affairs have placed greater emphasis on career development. Both Thompson Community College and Lucas Community College have dissolved their career services departments, and student activities have been asked to supplement some of those learning opportunities. Institutions have also placed a greater emphasis on what happens to students after they graduate. Lynn explained how gainful employment regulations have helped to reinforce the value of co-curricular education by demonstrating the marketability of students who take part in specific learning opportunities. As institutions put their efforts into the beginning and end of the student experience, less consideration is being given to what happens in the middle (the bulk of a student's experience).

Occupying a Minor Place in the Campus Completion Plan

Beginning in 2014, the Ohio Department of Higher Education required public colleges and universities to submit a Completion Plan every two years, the purpose of which is to "develop a systemic improvement approach for institution-wide policy and practice change, that reaches the department and classroom levels for direct impact on student persistence and completion" (OhioHigherEd, 2016, para. 1). Student development occupied a minor place in each participant's Campus Completion Plan or was absent entirely.

Within the Campus Completion Plans, co-curricular education and student development surfaced in very few instances. Bennington State College was the only institution to mention student activities directly. In other plans, such as that of Garfield Community College, student development was an outcome as part of a larger strategy. Most strategies that fell within the purview of the senior Student Affairs officer concerned retention, student support, or academic and career development. In addition, these strategies were almost always at the front-end of the student experience.

The ability to analyze updates from 2014 to 2016 provided further insight in that, aside from Garfield and Bennington State, co-curricular education and student development remained consistent or merited even less consideration. During follow-up conversations, participants acknowledged this deficiency and noted that it was something they were working to improve. The lack of strategies related to Student Affairs, and the sheer weight of strategies devoted to other facets of completion, suggest major changes need to take place to improve alignment between Student Affairs and overarching college priorities.

Limitations

Due to sampling measures, participants were diverse in terms of gender and experience but not race. Although the study did not seek to be representative of the population, a more diverse sample may have presented different insights. For instance, participants from a racial minority may have approached this topic from a critical lens, which this sample in general did not. While the lack of diversity was a random occurrence, different sampling measures could be put in place to ensure inclusion of diverse voices.

Discussion

Not unlike the widespread veneration of private enterprise within society, participants generally accepted the Completion Agenda's goals without concern for any adverse impact it might have on students. At the same time, almost every participant expressed a student development philosophy that championed the lifelong impact of co-curricular education and other student development opportunities. It is possible that participants did not feel they had agency to affect change at their institution, or that they view the Completion Agenda's goals and those within their own area as properly aligned. The following implications for practice can be adopted to allow Student Affairs educators to lead, even if they work within a framework that is bound by the current context.

Conversations about the Completion Agenda

The Completion Agenda is ubiquitous at community colleges. As this study demonstrated, completion impacts nearly every college decision but often goes undiscussed. In fact, the participants in this study each had a different understanding of the Completion Agenda, including when it came about and how it exists in its current form. It is imperative to have regular and ongoing discussions about the Completion Agenda from any area of the institution. Creating opportunities for sharing provides opportunities for reflection, critical insight, and engenders a sense of respect among educators with similar overall goals concerning student development and success.

Assessment Tied to Learning Outcomes

The need for Student Affairs to create a culture of evidence has existed for some time with varying levels of success (Oburn, 2005). Creating a culture of evidence is not an easy proposition, since finding appropriate evidence to substantiate co-curricular learning often lacks the empiricism found in curricular education. However, utilizing appropriate measures of effectiveness is precisely what will lend a certain level of authenticity to the work of Student Affairs.

Transparency

Sharing creates opportunities for a better understanding of Student Affairs practice. Once others better understand the value of Student Affairs, they are more likely to support those efforts. This process begins with achieving a similar level of transparency that has come to be expected from other areas of the institution (e.g., enrollment). In order to be recognized as an equally important part of the institution, Student Affairs divisions will need to purposefully collect data, package it, and share it with current and future partners.

Identifying Student Affairs Practice within the Student Experience

Pathways generalize the student experience and often oversimplify student intentions. Students are not always degree-seeking or decided when they enter an institution, and individuals encompass more than the credits they accumulate. Working within pathway constructs and identifying the intersections of progress and student development help to illustrate what competencies are developed at certain stages of the student experience. Student Affairs educators must better communicate their role within that process.

Maintaining the Core of the Profession

This study revealed a tendency for Student Affairs educators to be reactionary when confronted with external demands. Now, more than ever, it is vital that Student Affairs educators preserve what is essential about their work without compromising values. These values include

> ensuring access and opportunity for all, developing the whole student, providing quality services to meet student needs, believing that all students matter, facilitating student learning and success, and believing in the educational richness and power of the out-of-classroom environment.
>
> (Culp, 2005, p. 77)

Maintaining the core of the profession is critical to the other implications for practice having a significant impact.

Future research

Role of Completion Agenda Over Time

This study analyzed Student Affairs educators' beliefs about the Completion Agenda and its impact on their work during a specific timeframe. Since the Completion Agenda is not going away anytime soon, future studies would lend new insights and provide information on changing beliefs regarding the Completion Agenda and its impact on Student Affairs practice. A longitudinal study of campus completion plans or other improvement strategies could also yield interesting findings.

Student Experiences

Understanding the student perspective would offer a complete picture as it relates to developments in policy and practice. An anticipated challenge is that, since students are largely unaware of external forces shaping college decision-making, they may view their experiences as normal. With that said, the proper methodological approach could reveal insights that cannot be gained from staff or administrators. Also, studying cohorts of students would provide an opportunity to better understand systemic changes over time.

Conclusion

We approached this research with some concerns about the state of Student Affairs within the Completion Agenda. We were, therefore, surprised that participants overwhelmingly accepted changes taking place in Student Affairs practice. Findings from this study suggest that, without critical discussion, the Completion Agenda—and its largely economic goals—will continue unimpeded. Points of tension *do* exist, and educators need to be aware of these and respond appropriately. During a particularly enlightening discussion, Lynn said:

> If we believe Tinto's theory of [integration] and Astin's work on [involvement], if it helps to have students involved with each other and interacting in events, then you've got to have a way to tie that back to the outcomes that they came for and then also look at the benefits that they can derive, that maybe they didn't come for, but they need.

Without ignoring all the good that has come from better helping students reach their goals, Lynn was able to contest a narrative that student development needs to be convenient to be attractive. Like Lynn, all Student Affairs educators face a formidable challenge; they must respond to external expectations while holding true to professional values, a challenge that gets at the heart of Student Affairs work.

References

AACC. (2010). *Democracy's colleges: Call to action.* Washington, DC. Retrieved from http://www.aacc.nche.edu/newsevents/News/articles/Documents/callaction_04202010.pdf

ACPA. (1996). *The student learning imperative.* Retrieved from http://www.acpa.nche.edu/student-learning-imperative-implications-student-affairs

ACPA. (2014a). *The student personnel point of view (1937).* Retrieved from http://www.acpa.nche.edu/files/student-personnel-point-view-1937

ACPA. (2014b). *The student personnel point of view (1949).* Retrieved from http://www.acpa.nche.edu/student-personnel-point-view-1949

ACPA & NASPA. (2010). *Professional competency areas for student affairs practitioners.* Retrieved from https://www. naspa.org/images/uploads/main/Professional_Competencies.pdf

Astin, A. W. (1984). Student involvement: A developmental theory for higher education. *Journal of College Student Personnel, 25*(4), 297–308.

Astin, A. W. (1993). *What matters in college? Four critical years revisited.* San Francisco, CA: Jossey-Bass.

Astin, A. W. (1999). Student involvement: A developmental theory for higher education. *Journal of College Student Development, 40*(5), 518–529.

Bailey, T., Jaggars, S. S., & Jenkins, D. (2015). *Redesigning America's community colleges: A clearer path to student success.* Cambridge, MA: Harvard University Press.

Bernanke, B. S. (2008). *Remarks on Class Day 2008. Board of governors of the federal reserve system.* Cambridge, MA: Speech presented at Harvard University. Retrieved from http://www.federalreserve.gov/newsevents/speech/bernan ke20080604a.htm

Bragg, D. D., & Durham, B. (2012). Perspectives on access and equity in the era of (community) college completion. *Community College Review, 40*(2), 106–125.

Brinkmann, S., & Kvale, S. (2015). *Interviews: Learning the craft of qualitative research* (3rd ed.). Los Angeles, CA: SAGE.

Center for Community College Student Engagement. (2004). *Engagement by design.* Austin, TX: The University of Texas at Austin, Community College Leadership Program.

Center for Community College Student Engagement. (2008). *Starting Right: A first look at engaging entering students.* Austin, TX: The University of Texas at Austin, Community College Leadership Program.

Center for Community College Student Engagement. (2009). *Making connections: Dimensions of student engagement.* Austin, TX: The University of Texas at Austin, Community College Leadership Program.

Conley, D. T. (2008). *College knowledge: What it really takes for students to succeed and what we can do to get them ready.* San Francisco, CA: John Wiley & Sons.

Couturier, L. K. (2012). *Cornerstones of completion: State policy support for accelerated, structured pathways to college credentials and transfer. Jobs for the Future.* Completion by Design. Retrieved from http://www.jff.org/publications/cornerstones-completion-state-policy-support-accelerated-structured-pathways-college

Creamer, D. G. (1989). Changing internal conditions: Impact on student development. *New Directions for Community Colleges, 67,* 31–43.

Creswell, J. W. (2013). *Qualitative inquiry & research design: Choosing among five approaches* (3rd ed.). Thousand Oaks, CA: SAGE.

Creswell, J. W. (2014). *Research design: Qualitative, quantitative, and mixed methods approaches* (4th ed.). Thousand Oaks, CA: SAGE.

Culp, M. M. (2005). Doing more of what matters: The key to student success. *New Directions for Community Colleges, 131,* 77–87.

Dassance, C. R. (1984). Community college student personnel work: Is the model still emerging? *Community college review, 12*(3), 25–29.

Dassance, C. R. (2011). The next community college movement? *New Directions for Community Colleges, 156,* 31–39. doi:10.1002/cc.464

Elsner, P. A., & Ames, W. C. (1983). Redirecting student services. In G. B. Vaughan & Associates (Eds.), *Issues for community colleges leaders in a new era* (pp. 139–158). San Francisco, CA: Jossey-Bass.

Ferguson, J. (2010). The uses of neoliberalism. *Antipode, 41*(1), 166–184.

Floyd, D. L. (1991). *Toward mastery leadership: Issues and challenges for the 1990s.* Summary report of the Annual National Council on Student Development Leadership Colloquium (7th, Hilton Head, South Carolina, October 24–27, 1990).

Garrett, D., Bragg, D. D., & Makela, J. P. (2006). *Toward the future vitality of student development: The vision of the national council on student development.* Champaign, IL: National Council on Student Development, National Office, University of Illinois at Urbana-Champaign.

Hamer, J. F., & Lang, C. (2015). Race, structural violence, and the neoliberal university: The challenges of inhabitation. *Critical Sociology, 41*(6), 897–912.

Harbour, C. P., & Smith, D. A. (2016). The completion agenda, community colleges, and civic capacity. *Community College Journal of Research and Practice, 40*(2), 100–112. doi:10.1080/10668926.2014.996923

Hearn, J. C., & Rosinger, K. O. (2014). Socioeconomic diversity in selective private colleges: An organizational analysis. *Review of Higher Education, 38*(1), 71–104.

Helfgot, S. R. (1998). Introduction. In M. M. Culp & S. R. Helfgot (Eds.), *Life on the edge of the wave: Lessons from the community college* (pp. 1–9). Washington, DC: NASPA.

Helfgot, S. R. (2005). Core values and major issues in student affairs practice: What really matters? *New Directions for Community Colleges, 131,* 5–18.

Hirt, J. B. (2006). *Where you work matters: Student affairs administration at different types of institutions.* Lanham, MD: University Press of America.

Hughes, K. (2013). *The college completion agenda: 2012 progress report.* College Board Advocacy & Policy Center. Retrieved from http://media. collegeboard.com/digitalServices/pdf/advocacy/policycenter/college-completion- agenda-2012-progress-report.pdf

Jenkins, D., & Cho, S. W. (2013). Get with the program … and finish it: Building guided pathways to accelerate student completion. *New Directions for Community Colleges, 2013*(164), 27–35. doi:10.1002/cc.20078

Keyser, J. S. (1985). *1984 Traverse city statement: Toward the future vitality of student development services.* Retrieved from ERIC database. (ED260753).

Keyser, J. S. (1989). The student success systems model. In T. O'Banion (Ed.), *Innovation in the community college* (pp. 70–97). Retrieved from ERIC database (ED305981).

Lumina Foundation. (2013). *Strategic plan: 2013 to 2016*. Indianapolis, IN: Lumina. Retrieved from http://www. luminafoundation.org/advantage/document/goal_2025/2013-Lumina_Strategic_Plan.pdf

Malcolm, A. (2009). Full text of Obama's speech to congress and the nation. *Los Angeles Times*. Retrieved from http://latimesblogs.latimes.com/washington/2009/02/obama-text-spee.html

Marshall, C., & Rossman, G. B. (2011). *Designing qualitative research* (5th ed.). Los Angeles, CA: SAGE.

McClenney, K. (2013). To boost student success, make engagement inescapable. *Community College Week, 26*(8), 4–5.

Medsker, L. L. (1960). *Junior college: Progress and prospect*. New York, NY: McGraw-Hill.

Mellow, G. O., & Heelan, C. M. (2014). *Minding the dream: The process and practice of the American community college* (2nd ed.). Lanham, MD: Rowman & Littlefield.

Merriam, S. B. (1995). What can you tell from an N of 1?: Issues of validity and reliability in qualitative research. *PAACE Journal of Lifelong Learning, 4*, 51–60.

Merriam, S. B. (2002). Qualitative research in practice: Examples for discussion and analysis. San Francisco, CA: Jossey-Bass.

Merriam, S. B., & Tisdell, E. J. (2016). *Qualitative research: A guide to design and implementation* (4th ed.). San Francisco, CA: Jossey-Bass.

Mullin, C. M. (2010). *Rebalancing the mission: the community college completion challenge (Policy brief 2010–02PBL)*. American Association of Community Colleges. Retrieved from http://www.aacc.nche.edu/Publications/Briefs/ Pages/rb06152010.aspx

Munsch, P., & Cortez, L. (2014). Professional competencies for student affairs practice. *New Directions for Community Colleges, 166*, 47–53. doi:10.1002/cc.20101

National Conference for State Legislators. (2017). *Performance-based funding for higher education*. Retrieved from http://www.ncsl.org/research/education/performance-funding.aspx

O'Banion, T. (2010). The completion agenda: To what end? *Community College Journal, 81*(2), 44–47. Retrieved from http://www.3cmediasolutions.org/sites/default/files/TheCompletionAgendaToWhatEnd.pdf

O'Banion, T. (2011). Pathways to completion: Guidelines to boosting student success. *Community College Journal, 82*(1), 28–34.

O'Banion, T., Thurston, A., & Gulden, J. (1972). An emerging model. In T. O'Banion (Ed.), *New directions in community college student personnel programs* (pp. 7–14). Washington, DC: ACPA.

Oburn, M. (2005). Building a culture of evidence in student affairs. *New Directions for Community Colleges, 131*, 19–32. doi:10.1002/cc.203

Office of the Press Secretary. (2009). Remarks by the President on the American graduation initiative. *The White House.* Warren, MI: Speech presented at Macomb Community College. Retrieved from http://www.whitehouse.gov/ the_press_office/Remarks-by-the-President-on-the-American-Graduation-Initiative-in-Warren-MI

OhioHigherEd. Department of Higher Education. (2016). *Campus completion plans.* Retrieved from https://www. ohiohighered.org/campus-completion-plans

Ozaki, C. C. (2016). College impact theories past and present. *New Directions for Community Colleges, 174,* 23–33. doi:10.1002/cc.20200

Patton, M. Q. (2002). *Qualitative research & evaluation methods* (3rd ed.). Thousand Oaks, CA: SAGE.

Pennington, H., & Milliron, M. D. (2010). *Completion by design concept paper.* Seattle, WA: Bill & Melinda Gates Foundation. Retrieved from https://www.completionbydesign.org/s/article/Completion-by-Design-Concept-Paper- September-2010

Strange, C. (1994). Student development: The evolution and status of an essential idea. *Journal of College Student Development, 35*(6), 399–412.

Thorsen, D. E. (2010). The neoliberal challenge. What is neoliberalism? *Contemporary Readings in Law and Social Justice, 2*(2), 188–214.

Tinto, V. (1975). Dropout from higher education: A theoretical synthesis of recent research. *Review of Educational Research, 45*(1), 89–125.

Tinto, V. (1986), Theories of student departure revisited. In J. Smart (Ed.), *Higher education: Handbook of theory and research.* New York, NY: Agathon Press.

Tinto, V. (1993). *Leaving college: Rethinking the causes and cures of student attrition* (2nd ed.). Chicago, IL: Chicago University Press.

Tyrell, S. (2014). Creating and implementing practices that promote and support quality student affairs professionals. *New Directions for Community Colleges, 16,* 63–77. doi:10.1002/cc.20103

Vollmer, J. (2010). *Schools cannot do it alone: Building public support for America's public schools.* Fairfield, IA: Enlightenment Press.

Wang, X. (2017). Toward a holistic theoretical model of momentum for community college student success. In M. B. Paulsen (Ed.), *Higher education: Handbook of theory and research* (pp. 259–308). New York, NY: Springer.

Weissmann, J. (2012). Should science majors pay less for college than art majors? *The Atlantic.* Retrieved from https://www.theatlantic.com/business/archive/2012/11/should-science-majors-pay-less-for-college-than-art-majors/264417/

Welton, A., & Williams, M. (2015). Accountability, strain, college readiness drain: Sociopolitical tensions involved in maintaining a college-going culture in a high "minority," high poverty high school. *High School Journal, 98*(2), 184–204.

Wimbish, J., Bumphus, W. G., & Helfgot, S. R. (1995). Evolving theory informing practice. *New Directions for Student Services, 69,* 17–31.

Appendix A: Participant Table

Research study participants

Name	Gender	Race	Experience (years)	Institution	Administrator type
Aaron	Male	White	9	Putnam state	Student success
Alicia	Female	White	10	Garfield Northshore	Student affairs
Coline	Female	African American	14	Garfield downtown	Student affairs
Dario	Male	White	12	Trumbull	Student life
Dave	Male	White	25	Allen state	Student affairs
Debbie	Female	White	36	Highland	Student success
Erin	Female	White	8	Oakwood	Student affairs
Henry	Male	White	8	Lucas	Student life
Joseph	Male	White	15	Thompson	Student affairs
Kip	Male	White	8	Buck Creek	Student success
Lynn	Female	White	19	Garfield Northshore	Student affairs
Stacie	Female	White	31	Bennington state	Student life

Appendix B: Interview Protocol

Time of Interview:
Date:
Place:
Interviewer:
Interviewee:

Introductory Protocol: To facilitate note-taking, I would like to audio record our conversation today. For your information, only my Advisor for this the project and I will be privy to the tapes, which will be kept in a secure place until the completion of this project, at which time they will be destroyed. In addition, you must sign a consent to participate form, which outlines your participation in this project, the purpose, procedures, possible benefits, and potential risks. Your participation is voluntary, and you may stop at any time if you feel uncomfortable. I will give you a few minutes to review the consent to participate form. If you are willing, we will begin the interview process. (Allow interviewee to review and sign Consent to Participate form).

Interview Process: I have planned this interview to last no longer than one hour. During this time, I have several topics that I would like to cover, but the interview will be semi-structured, so we can move between topics based upon our conversation.

Description: This study is being done to learn more about what impact the Completion Agenda has had on co-curricular education at community colleges and how external forces have affected the work Student Affairs educators do with students. Your input is valued due to your current professional position at your institution and any experience you have in higher education related to this topic.

Interview Sections Used:
- A. Interviewee Background
- B. Completion Agenda Impact
- C. Value of Work
- D. Challenges Experienced
- E. Anticipated Challenges

(A) Interviewee Background

(B) Completion Agenda Impact
- (1) What is your understanding of the Completion Agenda? How do you define it?
- (2) When did you see it taking effect at your institution/in your role?
- (3) Do you feel the Completion Agenda has impacted your work with students? In terms of co-curricular education (defined here as any learning that takes place outside of the classroom)?
- (4) What overall impact do you feel the Completion Agenda has had at your institution?

(C) Value of Work
- (5) How would you describe the purpose of your profession?
- (6) Personally or professionally, how do you describe the value of your work?
- (7) Has the purpose of your profession/value you place on your work changed over time (from the start of the Completion Agenda until now)? What forces have affected it?
- (8) How do you believe others at your institution value your work?

(D) Challenges Experienced
- (9) Have you experienced any challenges between the value you place on your work and what is expected of you by others?
- (10) Do tensions exist between your work and larger institutional goals?

(E) Anticipated Challenges
   (11) What changes do you anticipate in your division in the next few years?
   (12) How do you see your area (Student Affairs, student services, etc.) changing?
   (13) In what ways do you envision co-curricular education to be impacted in the future by growing demands for completion?

Documents Obtained: _____

7   Elevating Student Affairs Practice in Community College Redesign

Michael A. Baston

The current national community college redesign effort, Guided Pathways, focuses on the need for "clearer, more educationally coherent programs of study that simplify students' choices without limiting their options" (Bailey, Jaggars, & Jenkins, 2015). Guided Pathways redesign efforts enable students to complete credentials and advance to further education and the labor market more quickly and at less cost. In an excellent primer on the subject, *Redesigning America's Community Colleges*, the authors Thomas Bailey, Shanna Jaggars, and Davis Jenkins (Bailey et al., 2015) noted that "community colleges were originally designed to expand college enrollments at low cost, not to maximize completion of high-quality programs of study" (Bailey et al., 2015). As a result, students picked courses from a "bewildering array of choices with little guidance" (Bailey et al., 2015) or self-reflection. The lack of structured guidance led to students changing majors multiple times, increasing the time and finances needed to complete a community college degree.

Community colleges engaged in redesign efforts are examining the way they offer programs and services, and restructuring these programs and services to put students in the best possible position to select and finish their course of study and transition to advance degrees or employment opportunities that provide a family-supporting wage. This article provides answers to some basic questions about the role of Student Affairs in the community college redesign effort commonly referred to as Guided Pathways. Specially, what is Guided Pathways? In what ways can Student Affairs contribute to this effort? How can Student Affairs collaborate with faculty in this initiative? How does it change our current work? What staffing and training is necessary?

What is Guided Pathways?

As noted, all too often, students begin their educational careers at community colleges with little to no knowledge of how to navigate the complexities of the college environment. They may have no sense of what their options or opportunities are at the college. Some make choices about their major with minimal information and perhaps solely influenced by current popular culture or the direction of a parent who has decided for the student what he or she should become in life. The lack of structure and strategy results in students taking six years to earn a two-year credential. Many earn excess credits, change majors multiple times, and run out of financial aid because of these choices, which then makes building student loan debt a matter of necessity rather than choice (Rosenbaum, Redline, & Stephan, 2007). According to data by the Center for Community College Student Engagement (CCCSE), this is especially true for many first-generation college students, ones who are the first in their family to go to college—some from a low socioeconomic background (Center for Community College Student Engagement, 2012). Guided Pathways, simply stated, is an institutional effort to create coherent academic and career pathways for students that leads to the student's intended goal of pursuing an advanced degree or transitioning into employment.

When community colleges choose to begin college redesign efforts, there are basic areas that are important for review. First, what are the regional talent needs in terms of future employment? This is important because academic programs should lead to positive labor market outcomes. Because some schools have many different majors, mapping academic programs, there is a course-taking sequence that helps students identify a recommended plan to finish. This includes guiding students to take the classes most appropriate to their goals, including gateway math, English, and other essential prerequisites. It also means that students who have to complete basic skill courses would do so in their first year of study. The ultimate objective is to get students on a path to the goals they have for themselves with the support to persist because time ultimately becomes the enemy of completion (Complete College America, 2011).

The literature on Student Affairs in the Guided Pathways approach is at a nascent stage. The role of Student Affairs in the Guided Pathways initiative largely focuses on the new student onboarding process and the need for intrusive advising with imbedded general discussions of career and transfer options. By limiting the role of Student Affairs in the Guided Pathways approach in this way, campus-based institutional approaches may miss critical opportunities to make college completion possible for community college students.

Student Affairs professionals are experienced design specialists. Focusing the profession on student learning, Student Affairs reframed the engagement paradigm (Calhoun, 1996). The most effective Student Affairs divisions perpetually design, realign, and recalibrate services to meet changing student needs throughout the entire student experience from recruitment to completion. While some senior Student Affairs officers may not have a full background in the emerging Guided Pathways movement in community colleges, many have implemented clear enrollment processes (Bontrager, 2004). They have also guided the design of effective approaches to career and academic advisement. Additionally, Student Affairs leaders know how to identify targeted student outcomes to include graduation, transfer, and the ability to obtain a career opportunity that leads to a family-supporting wage (Bailey et al., 2015). In learning from Student Affairs professionals, higher education is learning how to address social justice, equity, and inclusion (Bukowski, 2015). This contribution of this extensive body of work is essential in designing a successful and impactful Guided Pathways approach. Student Affairs executive teams must assert their professional expertise in all areas of the Guided Pathways initiative, or be limited to taking a reactionary posture following redesign. It is far more advantageous for community colleges when the division of Student Affairs is included in all efforts to inform and lead critical elements of change.

Where Do We Begin? The Student Experience as a Pathway

A good place to ground the work of Student Affairs in the Guided Pathways redesign is by looking at the entire student experience as a series of intentional exchanges. In *Understanding the Student Experience through the Loss/Momentum Framework: Clearing the Path to Completion*, the authors Elisa Rassen, Priyadarshini Chaplot, Davis Jenkins, and Rob Johnstone (Rassen, Chaplot, Jenkins, & Johnstone, 2013) defined the concept of the student experience as a "series of interactions between the student and the college"

(Rassen et al., 2013). For purposes of mapping a path to completion, the four key phases in the student's journey represent the Preventing Loss/Creating Momentum Framework. Those phases are:

- Connection (i.e., initial interest through submission of the application)
- Entry (i.e., enrollment through completion of gatekeeper courses)
- Progress (i.e., entry into course of study through completion of 75% of requirements)
- Completion (i.e., complete course of study through earning credential with labor market value).

Under the framework, students will either gain or lose momentum toward completion in part based on the interactions they have with the institution at any of the four identified critical phases. Policies, practices, programs, and processes, both within and external to the control of the institution, affect the phases (Rassen et al., 2013).

The work of Student Affairs connects to each aspect of the identified phases. For example, in the connection phase, the process of recruiting, training, and employing student ambassadors to guide potential students creates a valuable circular cycle of connection between both groups of students. The potential students gain college connections with their peers, while the student ambassadors gain skills for future success. Both the potential students and the ambassadors build momentum to matriculation through these connections and progress to degree is often increased. In the second phase, students at entry level, through new student orientation, comprehensive advising, first-year experience courses, and/or learning communities, are empowered to become members of the academic community. The academic learning center, with peer tutors and mentors, assists in the progress phase through knowledge acquisition and academic skill building. Likewise, effective Student Life programs increase student engagement and learning while targeted student service programs serving TRiO, Veterans, student parents, women, men of color, and students with disabilities increase the persistence and completion of historically underserved and marginalized populations. In the completion phase, assistance with transfer or entering the workforce supports students so they can complete their intended outcomes. In all of these phases, in more ways than articulated in this set of examples, Student Affairs provides comprehensive experiences and nonacademic supports that enable students to finish what they start and reach the goals they have for their future.

These critical phases, identified in the Loss/Momentum Framework, are also key points of influence in the Guided Pathways model. Student Affairs professionals hold a unique expertise in designing effective approaches to influencing student success at each stage of the student experience in college. Therefore, the role of Student Affairs in the institutional redesign toward a Guided Pathways model is essential.

Not Just a Faculty-Driven Initiative

Some community colleges have characterized Guided Pathways as a faculty-driven initiative. However, focusing redesign solely on course map sequencing is only a partial solution. An important aspect of creating coherence in the academic program is strategic recruitment into academic programs that align with transfer and labor market outcomes. The onboarding process redesign, often led by Student Affairs, should take into account, as part of that process, career exploration at the beginning of the student's matriculation. A newly designed Guided Pathways student advising and registration process must help students make informed program and course selections by utilizing innovative career services at the start of their journey at the college.

Proactive advising models also play a critical role in the Guided Pathways redesign. In order to best support students, the college must create intentional interactions with students to support their progress. This means monitoring student progress and identifying student behaviors that hinder their academic momentum and their ability to accumulate credits toward academic program completion. It is critical to address these concerns in real time.

This has not always been the community college approach to student support. The emphasis has often been on addressing the issues that students identify when they come to an office on their own or in response to a faculty referral as part of an early alert strategy. The connection with an advisor or counselor at this point is usually too late to salvage the student's semester because of its retrospective nature. Some community colleges are using segmentation strategies for students. They are dividing students into subsets and determining the interventions most appropriate for the subset. For example, some schools segment the students based on their credit accumulation. Supports could differ based on student status (0–15 credits, 16–30 credits, 31–45 credits, and 46+ credits). Others may have a different set of supports for full-time students than they do for part-time students. Some use grade point average as a basis for segmentation.

The goal of a segmentation strategy is to provide tailored guidance and support to students who need the specific interventions. The college or community partner can offer this guidance and support. In a time of limited resources and increasing needs, having the students connected to the appropriate resources and tracking the outcomes of that connection can reduce the number of students who, particularly for nonacademic reasons, stop or drop out. Student Affairs professionals know the student body that the campus serves. This knowledge can help in a segmentation process. Which students would benefit from high-tech, low-touch interventions? Those interventions would occur through text-messaging reminders or other nudging activities. Which kinds of students would benefit from much more high-touch, low-tech strategies because of the nature of the student's academic progress? Which students would benefit from peer interventions? Which students would benefit much more from a faculty or professional advisor connection? All of these realities make the expertise of Student Affairs professionals essential.

Helping students fund their college experience must be a part of Guided Pathways design. Knowing at the beginning how much money a student will need to achieve completion will enable the student to know, at what point in the experience, they will need additional funds. For example, students who have transferred to the community college from a prior institution, having already used financial aid, present the current institution with information that can help inform the student's educational finance plan. The financial aid advisors' expertise is central to the work of helping students complete the course of study.

Consider the student who works part-time. A financial aid advisor can help that student develop a budget based on their income. The financial aid advisor can then help the student strategize how to save part of their paycheck for the semesters where they will no longer be receiving financial aid. The financial aid advisor can also suggest that the college set up a savings account to receive the student's prepayments. The result is that the prepaid savings account can be applied to the bill in the semester where the student does not have financial aid.

Decisions about full-time and part-time attendance can be made intentionally with the help of financial aid advisors who can provide critical information. Questions such as what scholarships can assist to address gap semesters? and what about on-campus employment? are all questions that should inform the feasibility of staying on a path. Financial aid offices within Student Affairs can develop the capacity to provide models to students to answer these questions and to assist students in building financial literacy to make informed decisions about funding their education.

A path also should lead to somewhere. Student Affairs professionals' work in career and transfer services in redesign is key. The work of student engagement and involvement that provides students a variety of out-of-the-classroom experiences contextualizing in-class learning is also important. Employers want a skilled workforce. Applied learning opportunities offered by Student Affairs, through leadership development programs, service learning, and student government, help students develop the 21st-century skills necessary to gain a competitive advantage in the marketplace. What is clear is that the Guided Pathways redesign must be both a faculty- and staff-driven initiative. The contribution of Student Affairs throughout the entire student journey is vital.

Professional and Organizational Development in Redesign

The work of Guided Pathways will require professional development for Student Affairs professionals in different ways. The role of the Student Affairs professional will become more generalist in nature, and will be more cohort driven in terms of integrating supports and monitoring success outcome measures based on where the individual student is on their path. This means that technology will be integral in terms of communicating with students, monitoring their behaviors, and engaging them as they traverse their experience at the college. Informing Guided Pathways redesign, Student Affairs professionals must be knowledgeable and conversant about the language, role, and potential of technology. Understanding the college's enterprise resource planning platform, the student information system platform, the constituent relationship management platform, the learning management system platform, or any other technologic platform used to address enrollment management, student success, and/or instruction is essential. These platforms capture the data that enable the institution to understand how the student is responding to the college as a system, based on the way the student experiences the college. There are companies, often considered by community colleges in redesign, dedicated to taking the data from these various platforms to make predictions about students' success. Artificial intelligence is not a substitute for the expertise of Student Affairs; however, we must be skilled in our understanding and use of large amount of data and predictive analytics to avoid students being steered into academic programs that restrict their opportunity for future mobility based on an algorithm. Student Affairs involvement in the redesign effort must lead to discussions of the campus implications of technology on diversity, equity, and inclusion outcomes and initiatives.

The questions that we ask students will change. We will need to know more about the student's life outside of the college to assess factors that could lead them to stop or drop out. We will need to know if the student is employed, seeking employment, or employable because they will need resources to stay in school and experiences that will prepare them to enter into the next phase of their journey with the skills to succeed. We will need to ask more questions about the student's financing strategies for completion. We will also need to make sure students are on track to complete their chosen academic program of study. While these seem like simple questions, they require skill and training to elicit the information and to know the appropriate steps to help students succeed.

Redesign may require organizational structure changes. The approach to these changes will be greatly influenced by whether the college is in a union environment and working through the collective bargaining process or in a nonunion environment. The culture and organizational change resulting from a Guided Pathways redesign often requires revising job titles, creating new job descriptions, and establishing goal measures as part of the evaluation process. The clarity and spirit of collaboration and transparency within which the transition takes place will influence the likelihood of its success. In this regard, effective transformational leadership is imperative.

Conclusion

A successful Guided Pathways redesign requires a collective effort, college-wide buy-in, and the skills of transformational leaders. Senior Student Affairs officers have the capacity to play a critical role in this organizational change because of their expertise as experienced design specialists. Critical steps in the Guided Pathways model require intentional student engagement processes involving the work of Student Affairs areas. Therefore, any redesign effort must include leadership and participation from the Student Affairs division.

Likewise, Guided Pathways will require Student Affairs professionals to redefine roles, responsibilities, and approaches to their work. Student Affairs areas are constantly evolving and adapting to new trends and ideas. Early adopters of innovative technology or rapid response to new legislative policy directives demonstrate the structural agility of Student Affairs professionals to respond to barriers that impede student progress and address the immediacy of student issues and concerns. This agility enables Student Affairs practitioners to test interventions more nimbly and to design approaches for scale in ways that are more responsive to student needs.

Community colleges across the nation have adopted the Guided Pathways approach. Often, these redesign efforts are led by the Provost, or other institutional entities, while Student Affairs divisions are on the margins of the organizational change. Yet, the critical steps in the Guided Pathways approach center on the areas in which Student Affairs hold the greatest expertise. Promoting students' academic success requires that professionals working in Student Affairs have a clear understanding of how they will be involved in leveraging their expertise in student experience design and how they will be included in helping develop the plan for execution.

It is the responsibility of senior Student Affairs executives to make the case regarding the expertise Student Affairs brings to the Guided Pathways approach and in so doing, to open opportunities for both resource acquisition and broader institutional influence. Any redesign of the student experience without centering Student Affairs in this effort will prove unsuccessful. Now is the time to elevate the Student Affairs practice in community college redesign.

References

Bailey, T. R., Jaggars, S. S., & Jenkins, D. (2015). *Redesigning America's community colleges*. Cambridge, MA: Harvard University Press.

Bontrager, B. (2004). Strategic enrollment management: Core strategies and best practices. *College and University, 79*(4), 9–15.

Bukowski, J. (2015). Learning from student affairs professionals: Applying lessons of social justice, equity and inclusion in higher education administration. *The Vermont Connection, 36*, Article 13, 91–95.

Calhoun, J. C. (1996). The student learning imperative: Implications for student affairs. *Journal of College Student Development, 37*(2), 122–188.

Center for Community College Student Engagement. (2012). *A matter of degrees: Promising practices for community college student success (a first look).* Austin, TX: Community College Leadership Program, The University of Texas at Austin.

Complete College America. (2011). *Time is the enemy.* Indianapolis, IN: Complete College America.

Rassen, E., Chaplot, P., Jenkins, P. D., & Johnstone, R. (2013). *Understanding the student experience through the loss/momentum framework: Clearing the path to completion.* Sacramento: Completion by Design.

Rosenbaum, J. E., Redline, J., & Stephan, J. L. (2007). Community college the unfinished revolution. *Issues in Science and Technology, 23*(4), 49–56.

8 Preserving the Legacy of Dr. Jill Biden in a Post-Obama Era: Implications for Student Affairs Professionals at Community Colleges

Anne M. Hornak, C. Casey Ozaki, Amanda O. Latz, and Dan W. Royer

Community colleges have committed themselves to increase access to anyone wishing to engage in higher education. The community college-related work Dr. Jill Biden has accomplished in the last eight years is unprecedented, and her influence impacted all components of these institutions, including Student Affairs, where efforts are typically focused on the support of students at the margins in higher education. She has not only dedicated her career to teaching at a community college, but also taken the time to put community colleges in the forefront of national-level conversations about degree completion and workforce development, proclaiming that "community colleges are one of America's best-kept secrets" (The White House, n.d., para. 3). For community college professionals and scholars, preserving and advancing the advocacy work begun by Dr. Biden is important. Yet, the current presidential administration raises questions about how Dr. Biden's community college legacy of advocacy will continue to be enacted within Student Affairs.

How will the function, mission, and personnel within community college Student Affairs divisions be impacted by the 2017 change in the United States presidential administration? This scholarly essay, which addresses that question, has three parts. First, the authors outline the profound influence the Obama administration had on the community college landscape, giving specific attention to second lady Dr. Jill Biden's role. Next, the authors forecast how President Trump, his cabinet, and a shift in educational principles will affect community colleges broadly and Student Affairs specifically. Lastly, the authors offer concrete ways in which Student Affairs professionals within the community college sector can anticipate, reconcile, and respond to the coming changes. The authors emphasize the importance of the values infused within the Student Affairs profession (ACPA: College Student Educators International, n.d.), drawing attention to their inherent dissonance with underlying neoliberal market-driven principles. Through this comparison, the authors highlight the values of the Student Affairs profession and encourage institutional actors to preserve the legacy left by Dr. Jill Biden.

Community Colleges in the Obama–Biden Administration

Prior to the Obama administration and Dr. Biden's advocacy, community colleges have scarcely been a sole focus of national attention or federal policy and funding. President Obama tapped Biden as a key figure to represent the administration in its interests and goals with regard to community college education. A highlight of Dr. Biden's work was the White House Summit on Community Colleges (Biden, 2011). Spearheaded by Dr. Biden, the Summit was the first-ever, national conversation focused on community colleges and their role in contributing to economic mobility in America. Emboldened by President Obama's challenge for the United States to produce 5 million community college graduates by 2020 (Biden, 2011), the Summit gathered community college presidents, students, faculty, and scholars, in addition to individuals from the philanthropic community, policy experts, and state and federal lawmakers with interests in community college policy,

> [t]o emphasize the role of community colleges in achieving the President's goal of making America the most educated country in the world . . . [and] to demonstrate that community colleges are critical partners in our efforts to prepare our graduates to lead in the 21st century workforce.
>
> (Biden, 2011, p. 7)

There were three initiatives announced at the Summit (Biden, 2011). First, the "Skills for America's Future" initiative aimed at improving industry and community college partnerships, with a goal to build a nationwide network. Second, a $34.8 million grant competition funded by the Bill & Melinda Gates Foundation to promote new approaches to making schools more responsive to students. And, finally, a $1 million Aspen Institute prize for community college excellence. Furthermore, within the year following the Summit, four regional community college summits were held across the country, with a culminating *Community College Virtual Symposium* event.

While it is difficult to point to the long-term impact of the 2010 Summit for Student Affairs and services, there have been some tangible outcomes, such as the Gates Foundation's *Completion by Design* program, which became a pioneer for the development and implementation of Guided Pathways for students (Bailey, Jaggars, & Jenkins, 2015). These Pathways focus on bringing together academic and student support services and are having an impact, for example, on advising, mentoring, intervention strategies, orientation, and career advising. Another significant initiative concurrently initiated in response to President Obama's challenge was the American Association for Community Colleges' 21st Century Initiative (American Association of Community Colleges [AACC], 2012), which included a listening tour, a commission report (American Association of Community Colleges, 2012) and implementation guide (American Association of Community Colleges, 2014), and the work of 112 community college leaders to develop strategies and model action plans to guide community colleges in achieving the goals outlined in the report. While not specific to student services, these initiatives are prompting and guiding academic and support services to reexamine the process of educating and graduating community college students. The focus on community colleges during the Obama administration not only promoted the visibility of these institutions but also advanced a new sense of attention, appreciation, and validation for community colleges and the criticality of their role in higher education—and beyond.

Community College Student Affairs During the Trump Administration

The difficulty in keeping the momentum created during the Obama administration and by Dr. Biden is that the new president has not expressed attention to or urgency around these important initiatives. During his 18-month presidential campaign, Donald Trump rarely talked about higher education, and when he did, it was included as subtext in polices that would limit access [e.g., immigration policies, rhetoric that further marginalizes already minoritized current and prospective students (Morgan, 2017)]. Furthermore, the new Secretary of Education Betsy DeVos's focus and experience has been on school vouchers and increasing choice for K-12 students. Therefore, without much of a precedent, it is unclear how this will impact higher education, and, namely, community college Student Affairs professionals. Yet, there are indicators in the early months of the Trump administration of what community colleges, and specifically their Student Affairs units, might expect.

At this point, projection as to how the new administration might affect the role of community colleges is at the broad policy and orientation level with ideas for direct and indirect influence on student services. Having a free market and competition-based economy and society have been the overriding goals guiding Trump's administration in their decision-making to date. Assuming that this orientation continues, the authors can expect an increased focus on community colleges as a good financial deal (e.g., education for cost) and critical in growing the job market.

One consequence of the new administration's orientation to higher education could be a resurgence of competition between community colleges and for-profit institutions. Obama-era regulations were designed to hold for-profit colleges accountable and provide loan relief if students were victims of fraud or misrepresentation by their institutions. First, the Gainful Employment Regulation requires institutions to demonstrate that their graduates' incomes allow them to pay back their student loans (U.S. Department of Education, 2014). This is a particular problem among for-profit institutions that make misleading employment promises on which they cannot deliver (Belfield, 2016). Second, the Bower Defense to Repayment regulation provides guidelines for how defrauded student loan borrowers can apply for loan forgiveness (U.S. Department of Education, 2016). By summer 2017, the US Department of Education was processing 16,000 loan forgiveness claims (Harris, 2017a), costing in the upward of $500 million. During the Obama administration, a federal "shopping sheet" was created for students to compare financial aid packages across multiple institutions to truly understand an aid package (Grasgreen, 2015). Safeguards like this are being rolled back or put on hold, by the current administration and stand to be nonexistent within a few years (The Guardian, 2017).

Deregulation and easing of these safeguards and restrictions would allow for more unfettered growth and influence in the market. In addition, community colleges may welcome a renegotiation of the gainful employment rule, which was found to be onerous for these institutions (Harris, 2017a). In DeVos's confirmation hearing, she would not commit to protecting or enforcing the gainful employment rules, raising the question of the administrations' priorities—do they value competition overprotecting and overseeing the interests of the student (Douglas-Gabriel, 2017)? The gainful employment rule requires colleges to track their graduates' performance, following graduation, in the workforce. The goal is to cut off federal funding for colleges that are awarding degrees that are essentially worthless in the marketplace, but graduates are strapped with insurmountable debt (Grasgreen, 2015). Furthermore, on the campaign trail, Trump said "reducing regulation would clear a path for schools to cut administrative staff and lower their costs" (Clark, Daugherty, & Mulhere, 2016, para. 20). This appears to be playing out more recently through DeVos's controversial decision to roll back these regulations—welcomed by some and found concerning and unfair by others (Harris, 2017a, 2017b). DeVos contended that these regulations are creating "a muddled process that's unfair to students and schools and puts taxpayers on the hook for significant costs" (The Guardian, 2017, para. 5).

A tide turning toward deregulation, increased competition, and reducing administration and staff would impose a heavy burden of potential changes on Student Affairs professionals. First, community colleges have historically been America's colleges—democratic, open access, and vehicles of equity. The student development role of Student Affairs in an equity-minded, democratic system is clearly aligned with the goals of supporting students through their educational careers. In a competition-based, outcomes-oriented, capitalist educational environment, the role of Student Affairs is likely to change to one more narrowly focused on enrollment management, recruiting, branding, and marketing. The authors are likely to see an ever-increasing presence of what Lee and Helm (2013) called Student Affairs capitalism. Second, in a competitive environment, overall resources are likely to follow these values. One implication is that funds and positions would shift to these areas of focus, resulting in a reduction of Student Affairs positions. Another is that the producers, a metaphor for community college Student Affairs professionals coined by Hirt (2006), will be made to produce even more—without compensation—and to the detriment of any time and/or efforts meant to foster student support, development, and learning. Compounding and reinforcing these potential projections for how Student Affairs might be affected by changing values in the new administration is the current educational context of accountability for completion outcomes, most recently states tying those outcomes to funding. This environment increasingly puts pressure on community colleges and their Student Affairs units to demonstrate the impact it plays on student learning and completion; a deregulated and more competitive higher education climate could amplify the expectation and need to perform.

Response and Action

Lastly, the authors offer concrete ways in which Student Affairs professionals within the community college sector can anticipate, reconcile, and respond to the coming changes. Some of the largest changes will most likely be felt within the financial markets and how the stock market responds to this administration. This is largely out of the control of Student Affairs professionals, but financial aid professionals may be impacted and may choose to think about how they talk to prospective families regarding financing college. The impact of deregulation may have a much deeper impact on community college Student Affairs professionals. If President Trump follows Republican lawmakers' campaigning for deregulation, the administrative capacities related to compliance may be in jeopardy. This may have bigger implications for offices that provide services related to equity and safety on the campuses (i.e., Title IV compliance and financial aid regulations; Title IX compliance; grant-funded programs for underserved students).

The authors encourage Student Affairs professionals within the community college sector to consider the following. First, Student Affairs professionals will need to prepare to operate within an increasingly ambiguous and rapidly changing regulatory environment. To do this will require institutions to build a knowledge and skill capacity that may be new to a profession that has often relied on leadership, psychological, cognitive, and managerial development to socialize, educate, and prepare its new professionals. The future may expect professionals to become increasingly savvy on how to operate within a political environment that is more business-oriented and potentially politically unfriendly. To be functional and, ideally, effective within this environment Student Affairs units can recruit and hire (new) professionals from graduate-level Student Affairs preparation programs, and, ideally, these applicants will possess some training and/or backgrounds in business-oriented principles. Furthermore, internal professional development that supports both the internationalization of Student Affairs principles and a fluid understanding business and competition-based goals can assist professionals to be responsive to changing environment while maintaining a student-centered foundation. Effective practitioners will be grounded in the field's guiding principles as well as the current set of contexts in which they operate (e.g., institutional, state, federal). A critical part of this selective responsiveness to the environment is the need to encourage institutional leadership to engage and develop communication with stakeholders (e.g., students, faculty, community) that aligns with the institutional mission statement, which may conflict with federal-level policies and gestures. Leadership and Student Affairs professionals must continue to listen to stakeholders, while also taking advantage of the opportunity to inform and influence them about the goals and purposes of community colleges.

Second, for many, the community college setting may be a safer and more supportive environment compared to other settings, but the unpredictability of the Trump administration's educational and social policy can produce more uncertainty and vulnerability for many students, staff, and faculty. In addition, as emotions run high in this political environment, college campuses are not immune to the volatility of a hostile climate. As professionals educated and responsible for supporting and creating inclusive campuses for all, they may not only be in positions to affect and influence campus, but the campus community may turn to these professionals for leadership and modeling. This positioning is also an opportunity to encourage candid conversations about the political environment among colleagues, centrally focused on what is best for students, particularly students who have been and/or are currently marginalized within society for any of a number of reasons (e.g., socioeconomic status, race, sexual orientation, gender identity).

It is important for Student Affairs professionals to continue to recognize that the current political environment disproportionately targets and negatively affects individuals who typically represent a majority population in the community college arena and consider what this means for practice. For example, undocumented students are a sizable and often invisible on population on community college campuses. The recent announcement by the Trump administration to rescind the Deferred Action for Childhood Arrivals (DACA) program threatens the livelihood and safety of the students enrolled in this program. The depth of fear, anxiety, and uncertainty that these students are experiencing post-decision may be onerous and oppressive.

Based on the field's guiding principles, Student Affairs professionals will continue to demonstrate support and action for undocumented and DACA students. Following the DACA announcement, Susana Muñoz (2017) made a series of suggestions for how institutions can respond to and support these students. First, talk to students directly, listen to their stories, and ask them what they need to feel safe and supported, advocating for their needs to be institutional priorities. Second, encourage professionals and student organizations on campus to program around immigration rights issues. This provides fodder to promote campus dialogs and genesis for policy development. Third, providing easy access to information (e.g., website) and resources that students might need to navigate their future is an important embodiment of allyship. In addition, campuses should have a plan in place to address potential intersection with immigration, customs, and enforcement and can be led by the student services units, determining how to best protect its students. Finally, the emotional and active labor of working with these targeted and vulnerable students at community colleges can be taxing and exhausting. Therefore, professionals need to engage in professional boundary setting, self-care, and peer support. Furthermore, engaging in shared education on the topic, in addition to shared labor, will allow for a more impactful and sustainable deeply emotional and consequential work.

The fate and work of Student Affairs professionals of community colleges during the Trump administration era remains to be seen, though indicators from the first year suggest that deregulation, increased competition, and a reduction of staff and administration are likely in the future. In this context, Student Affairs professionals will likely have to reexamine the role community colleges play in educating students. The landscape of higher education is impacted significantly by the federal government, opposed to the K-12 system, which is largely state run, so having an administration that does not fully embrace and understand the mission of community colleges could have a major impact on all components of the institution—beyond Student Affairs. Initially, colleges may not fully realize these potential changes; however, with increasing deregulation and a free market approach to education, students with insurmountable debt and degrees considered "worthless" upon graduation may look to community colleges for assistance in degree completion or retraining (Grasgreen, 2015). Much of this debate is still unfolding with the impact on community colleges unknown, as Student Affairs preparation faculty consider how to prepare students to work at community colleges, looking at the legacy of Dr. Jill Biden and the Obama administration offers a powerful counter-narrative to the rhetoric and actions of current administration. Perhaps more so than ever before, the authors must look to their democracy's colleges to lead the way in providing higher education access to their country's most minoritized persons. While not an inherent threat to this end, leveraging community college solely for their capacity to prepare individuals to contribute to a capitalist economy has consequences—some of which can be negative. For example, one consequence could be a shrinkage of the community college's transfer mission. Finally, the authors encourage a critical version of hope—one that believes in a better tomorrow while seeing clearly the challenges of today.

References

ACPA: College Student Educators International. (n.d.). *Statement of ethical principles & standards*. Retrieved from http://www.myacpa.org/sites/default/files/Ethical_Principles_Standards.pdf

American Association of Community Colleges. (2012). *Reclaiming the American dream: Community colleges and the nation's future*. Washington, DC: Author. Retrieved from http://www.aacc21stcenturycenter.org

American Association of Community Colleges. (2014). *Empowering community colleges to build the nation's future: An implementation guide*. Washington, DC: Author. Retrieved from www.aacc21stcenturycenter.org

Bailey, T. R., Jaggars, S. S., & Jenkins, D. (2015). *Redesigning America's community colleges: A clearer path to student success*. Cambridge, MA: Harvard University Press.

Belfield, C. (2016, October 12). *Comparing closed for-profit colleges to the public college sector*. Retrieved from http://capseecenter.org/comparing-closed-for-profit-colleges-to-public-college-sector/

Biden, J. (2011). Remarks by the President and Dr. Jill Biden at the White House summit on community colleges. *The White House summit on community colleges summit report*. Washington, DC. Retrieved from https://obamawhite house.archives.gov/sites/default/files/uploads/community_college_summit_report.pdf

Clark, K., Daugherty, G., & Mulhere, K. (2016, November 9). What Trump's election means or college students and parents. *Time*. Retrieved from http://time.com/money/4564513/what-trumps-election-means-for-college-students-and-parents/

Douglas-Gabriel, G. (2017, February 8). How will DeVos influence higher education? *The Washington Post*. Retrieved from https://www.washingtonpost.com/news/grade-point/wp/2017/02/08/how-will-devos-influence-higher-education/?utm_term=.8d6d8135e288

Grasgreen, A. (2015). Obama pushes for-profit colleges to the brink. *Politico*. Retrieved from http://www.politico.com/story/2015/07/barack-obama-pushes-for-profit-colleges-to-the-brink-119613

The Guardian. (2017). Eighteen states sue Betsy DeVos for suspending rules on for-profit colleges. *The Guardian.* Retrieved from https://www.theguard ian.com/us-news/2017/jul/06/betsy-devos-lawsuit-for-profit-colleges

Harris, A. (2017a, June 14). DeVos will roll back 2 Obama regulations, a blow to consumer advocates. *The Chronicle of Higher Education.* Retrieved from http://www.chronicle.com/article/DeVos-Will-Roll-Back-2-Obama/240337

Harris, A. (2017b, June 23). What DeVos's 'reset' on 2 major consumer rules means for colleges. *The Chronicle of Higher Education, 63*(39). Retrieved from http://www.chronicle.com/article/What-DeVos-s-Reset-on/240348

Hirt, J. B. (2006). *Where you work matters: Student affairs administration at different types of institutions.* Lanham, MD: University Press of America.

Lee, J. J., & Helm, M. (2013). Student affairs capitalism and early-career student affairs professionals. *Journal of Student Affairs Research and Practice, 50*, 290–307.

Morgan, J. (2017). A new frontier: US academia under President Trump. *The world university rankings.* Retrieved from https://www.timeshigher education.com/features/new-frontier-us-academia-under-president-trump

Muñoz, S. (2017, September 5). An open letter to college presidents about DACA. *Diverse Issues in Higher Education.* Retrieved from http://diver-seeducation.com/article/101138/

U.S. Department of Education. (2014, October 31). Final regulations. *Federal Register, 79*(211), 64890–65103. Retrieved from https://ifap.ed.gov/fregisters/attachments/FR103114Final.pdf

U.S. Department of Education. (2016, November 1). Final regulations. *Federal Register, 81*(211), 75926–76089. Retrieved from https://www.gpo.gov/fdsys/pkg/FR-2016-11-01/pdf/2016-25448.pdf

The White House. (n.d.). *Dr. Jill Biden.* Retrieved from https://www.white house.gov/administration/jill-biden

Index

Printed in the United States
by Baker & Taylor Publisher Services